Jane Borthwick, S. L. Findlater

Hymns from the land of Luther

Jane Borthwick, S. L. Findlater

Hymns from the land of Luther

ISBN/EAN: 9783742835819

Manufactured in Europe, USA, Canada, Australia, Japa

Cover: Foto ©Angelika Wolter / pixelio.de

Manufactured and distributed by brebook publishing software (www.brebook.com)

Jane Borthwick, S. L. Findlater

Hymns from the land of Luther

HYMNS

FROM THE

Land of Luther

TRANSLATED FROM THE GERMAN

BY

H. L. L.

FIFTEENTH THOUSAND.

LONDON.
T. NELSON AND SONS, PATERNOSTER ROW.
EDINBURGH; AND NEW YORK.

1884.

Preface.

It is now a number of years since the "Hymns from the Land of Luther" were given to the public, in four separate series, afterwards collected into one volume. For some time this work has been out of print. The present edition includes all the four series, revised and corrected, with the addition, by the same translator, of a selection from the poems of the late talented Swiss poetess, Meta Heusser, under the title of "Alpine Lyrics."

Some of the hymns cannot be called very literal translations, but rather aim at conveying the general idea and spirit of the German verses in an English form. One poem, "The Desired Haven"—which is not a translation—was by mistake printed at first among the others; and having proved a favourite with most readers, it is retained "under protest."

H. L. L.

Edinburgh, 1884.

Contents.

HYMNS FROM THE LAND OF LUTHER.

JOYS TO COME,	13
DYING PETITIONS,	15
WEEP NOT,	18
HERE IS MY HEART,	21
DISCIPLINE,	24
JESUS, STILL LEAD ON,	26
TO A DYING CHILD,	28
ARISE!	30
GOD WITH ME,	33
THE COMMUNION OF SAINTS,	35
EVENING HYMN,	38
MY GOD! I KNOW THAT I MUST DIE,	41
LIGHT IN DARKNESS,	43
LET ME FIND THEE!	46
GRIEF AND CONSOLATION BY A MOTHER'S DEATH-BED,	48
AH! GRIEVE NOT SO,	50
PILGRIM SONG,	52
MY FATHER IS THE MIGHTY LORD,	55

CONTENTS.

THY WILL BE DONE,	57
THE GOOD SHEPHERD,	60
REJOICE,	62
THE ANGEL AND THE INFANT,	65
THE SERVICE OF THE LORD,	67
THE DESIRED HAVEN,	69
THE LONG GOOD-NIGHT,	71
ALL THINGS ARE YOURS,	73
THE WIDOW OF NAIN,	75
CONFLICT,	77
LOVE TO CHRIST,	80
PARTING,	82
THE ANGEL OF PATIENCE,	84
LOOKING HOME,	86
MORNING HYMN,	88
RECALL,	90
GOING HOME,	93
THE JOURNEY TO JERUSALEM,	95
THE MERCHANT,	97
SUBMISSION,	100
WAITING,	102
PRAISE AND PRAYER,	104
CALVARY,	107
RE-UNION,	110
JESUS ALL-SUFFICIENT,	112
ANTICIPATION,	114
"GOD CALLING YET,"	116
RESIGNATION,	118
REST,	120
LOOKING TO JESUS,	122
PRAISE,	124
HYMN SUNG AT A FUNERAL,	126

CONTENTS.

RESURRECTION,	128
HERE AND THERE,	130
JOY IN BELIEVING,	133
LOWLY,	135
THE CHRISTIAN CROSS,	138
SONG OF THE SOJOURNER,	139
THE CHRISTIAN HOUSEHOLD,	142
THE TWO JOURNEYS,	144
SHADOW AND SUBSTANCE,	146
THE MISSIONARY ON THE SEA-SHORE,	148
SABBATH MORNING HYMN,	150
CHARITY,	152
WE TOO ARE THINE,	154
SUBMISSION,	157
A PASTOR'S PARTING WORDS,	161
BE THOU MY FRIEND,	163
AS THOU WILT,	166
SABBATH HYMN,	168
WHAT PLEASES GOD,	170
AT LAST,	172
THE GRAVEYARD,	174
FUNERAL HYMN,	176
MINISTERING ANGELS,	178
THE MIDNIGHT CRY,	180
YET THERE IS ROOM,	182
COMFORT,	185
THE MISSIONARY'S FAREWELL,	187
THE SHEPHERDS,	189
MORNING HYMN,	190
EVENING HYMN,	193
THE LITTLE FLOCK,	196
OUR ELIZA,	199

CONTENTS.

EASTER HYMN,	201
"WE ARE THE LORD'S,"	203
LOVE AND THE CROSS,	205
MY BELOVED IS MINE, AND I AM HIS,	207
"ONE THING IS NEEDFUL,"	209
CONFESSION,	211
GRATITUDE,	212
PRAYER,	214
THE FATHER KNOWS THEE,	216
JESUS THE WAY,	218
COMMUNION,	220
THOU KNOWEST THAT I LOVE THEE,	223
THE MORNING OF JOY,	225
THE TWO CALLS,	227
WARFARE,	229
JESUS ONLY,	232
THE CROSS,	234
THE SONG OF SONGS,	237
MORNING IN SPRING,	238
THE CALL OBEYED,	241
SABBATH MORNING,	243
REMEMBER ME,	245
PEACE,	248
WALKING IN LIGHT,	250
FUNERAL HYMN,	252
LIGHT IN DARKNESS,	254
CHRISTMAS HYMN,	256
REDEEMING LOVE,	257
THE PRINCE OF LIFE,	259
PRAYER AND SUPPLICATION,	261
SACRAMENTAL HYMN,	263
THINGS NEW AND OLD,	265

ALPINE LYRICS.

MOUNTAINS,	269
UNDER THE STARS,	272
AT MIDNIGHT,	276
THEODORA,	279
ALONE AT EVENING,	281
TO MY YOUNGEST CHILD, ON HER CONFIRMATION DAY,	283
TO A NAME-CHILD BEYOND THE SEA,	286
DAVID AND JONATHAN,	289
THE BROOK,	291
EASTER HYMN,	293
PILGRIM SONG,	297
PILGRIM PRAYERS,	299
"PRECIOUS IN THE SIGHT OF THE LORD IS THE DEATH OF HIS SAINTS,"	301
PARTING FROM TWO YOUNG FRIENDS,	304
THE FIRST STEP,	306
AN EVENING TALE,	308
WORDS OF CHEER,	310
"NOT ONE OF THEM IS FORGOTTEN BEFORE GOD,"	313
"IN EVERY THING GIVE THANKS,"	316
FAREWELL TO A FOREIGN MISSIONARY,	318
HYMN,	321
AN AUTUMN EVENING,	324
AFTER MANY FAREWELLS,	327
GOLDAU,	329
LAST PRAYERS,	332
"OUT OF THE DEPTHS,"	334
ON A DARK WINTER DAY,	336
"A LITTLE WHILE,"	339

CONTENTS.

EVENING MUSINGS,	341
BE STILL!	343
SPRING,	345
FALLING ASLEEP,	347
FOR EVER WITH THE LORD!	348

HYMNS FROM THE LAND OF LUTHER.

JOYS TO COME.

"Wird das nicht Freude seyn?"

Will that not joyful be,
When we walk by faith no more,
When the Lord we loved before,
   As Brother-man we see;
When He welcomes us above,
When we share His smile of love,
   Will that not joyful be?

Will that not joyful be,
When to meet us rise and come
All our buried treasures home,
   A gladsome company!
When our arms embrace again
Those we mourned so long in vain,
   Will that not joyful be?

JOYS TO COME.

    Will that not joyful be,
When the foes we dread to meet,
Every one, beneath our feet
    We tread triumphantly!
When we never more can know
Slightest touch of pain or woe,
    Will that not joyful be?

    Will that not joyful be,
When we hear what none can tell,
And the ringing chorus swell
    Of angels' melody!
When we join their songs of praise,
Hallelujahs with them raise,
    Will that not joyful be?

    Yes! that will joyful be!
Let the world her gifts recall,
There is bitterness in all;
    Her joys are vanity;
Courage, dear ones of my heart!
Though it grieves us here to part,
    There, we will joyful be!

               H. C. von Schweinitz.

DYING PETITIONS.

"*Gedenke mein, mein Gott!*"

"Remember me, my God! remember me
  In hour of deepest woe;
Thou art my only hope, my only plea,
  Against th' accusing foe.
Oh, show me now Thy full salvation,
Oh, hear my dying supplication!
      Remember me!"

"I think on thee, believer! tremble not,
  Thy Saviour still is near:
Here is My cross, My blood to cleanse each spot,
  My promises to cheer.
Is not My love unchanged, unshaken?
Mine own shall never be forsaken—
      I think on thee!"

"Remember me! man's help can nought avail
  In the dark valley's shade;
My strength must faint, my flesh and heart must fail,
  Oh, haste Thou to mine aid!

Silence and darkness o'er me stealing,
Oh, be Thou still Thyself revealing,—
      Remember me!"

"I think on thee! soon in the better land
  Thou shalt with Me rejoice;
The harps of heaven are waiting for thy hand,
  The chorus for thy voice;
The angel bands are round thee bending,
Thy parting spirit close attending,—
      I think on thee!"

"Remember me! by Thine own hour of pain,
  Appear in mine to save!
Smooth for my rest the couch where Thou hast lain,
  The pillow of the grave;
And while the years of time are flying,
In that lone place of darkness lying,—
      Remember me!"

"I think on thee! thine own Redeemer lives,
  Thy hope shall not be vain:
When the last trump its solemn summons gives,
  Thou shalt arise again.
Now, go in peace, securely sleeping,
Thy dust is safe in angels' keeping,—
      I think on thee!"

"Remember me, and the afflicted band
    Whom I must leave behind!
Pour consolation from Thine own rich hand
    On mourning heart and mind.
Oh, hear this one, this last petition!
Then shall I go in glad submission,—
                Remember me!"

"I think on thee! with that sad band of love
    I will in mercy deal;
My tender sympathy their souls shall prove,
    My Spirit's power to heal.
The long-sought bliss shall yet be given,
The lost of earth are found in heaven,—
                I think on thee!"

CHORUS OF THE CHURCH.

"Now, sweetly sleep! angels thy soul receive,
    And bear to Jesus' breast!
Long in our hearts thy memory shall live;
    Here let thy body rest,
Secure from earthly pain and sorrow,
Till dawns the resurrection morrow.
                Now, sweetly sleep!"

UNBEKANNTES.

WEEP NOT.

"Weine nicht!"

Weep not,—Jesus lives on high,
   O sad and wearied one!
If thou with the burden sigh
   Of grief thou canst not shun,
          Trust Him still,—
         Soon there will
Roses in the thicket stand,
Goshen smile in Egypt's land.

Weep not,—Jesus thinks of thee
   When all beside forget,
And on thee so lovingly
   His faithfulness has set,
          That though all
         Ruined fall,
Everything on earth be shaken,
Thou canst never be forsaken.

WEEP NOT.

Weep not,—Jesus heareth thee,
  Hears thy moanings broken,
Hears when thou right wearily
  All thy grief hast spoken.
      Raise thy cry,
      He is nigh,
And when waves roll full in view,
He shall fix their "Hitherto."

Weep not,—Jesus loveth thee,
  Though all around may scorn,
And though poisoned arrows be
  Upon thy buckler borne,
      From His love,
      Nought can move;
All may fail,—yet only wait,
He shall make the crooked straight.

Weep not,—Jesus cares for thee.
  Then what of good can fail?
Why shouldst thou thus gloomily
  At thought of trouble quail?
      He will bear
      All thy care;
And if He the burden take,
He will all things perfect make.

WEEP NOT.

Weep not,—Jesus comforts thee;
 Soon shall He come and save,
And each sorrow thou shalt see
 Lie buried in thy grave.
  Sin shall die,
  Grief shall fly,
Thou hast wept thy latest tears,
When the Lord of life appears!

B. Schmolk.

HERE IS MY HEART.

"Hier ist mein Herz."

Here is my heart!—my God, I give it Thee:
 I heard Thee call and say,
"Not to the world, my child, but unto Me,"—
 I heard, and will obey.
 Here is love's offering to my King,
 Which in glad sacrifice I bring—
  Here is my heart.

Here is my heart!—surely the gift, though poor,
 My God will not despise.
Vainly and long I sought to make it pure,
 To meet Thy searching eyes:
 Corrupted first in Adam's fall,
 The stains of sin pollute it all—
  My guilty heart!

Here is my heart!—long time so hard and cold,
 Now softened by Thy grace,

It seeks, in lowly sorrow, to behold
    Thy reconciled face.
It groans beneath the weight of sin,
It sighs salvation's joy to win—
      My mourning heart!

Here is my heart!—in Christ its longings end,
    Near to His cross it draws;
It says, "Thou art my portion, O my Friend,
    Thy blood my ransom was."
And in the Saviour it has found
What blessedness and peace abound,—
      My trusting heart!

Here is my heart!—ah! Holy Spirit, come,
    Its nature to renew,
And consecrate it wholly as Thy home,
    A temple fair and true.
Teach it to love and serve Thee more,
To fear Thee, trust Thee, and adore,—
      My cleansed heart!

Here is my heart!—it trembles to draw near
    The glory of Thy throne;
Give it the shining robe Thy servants wear,
    Of righteousness Thine own:

Its pride and folly chase away,
And all its vanity, I pray,—
      My humbled heart!

Here is my heart!—teach it, O Lord, to cling
    In gladness unto Thee;
And in the day of sorrow still to sing,
    "Welcome, my God's decree."
Believing, all the journey through,
That Thou art wise, and just, and true,—
      My waiting heart!

Here is my heart!—O Friend of friends, be near
    To make each tempter fly;
And when my latest foe I wait with fear,
    Give me the victory!
Gladly on Thy love reposing,
Let me say, when life is closing,
      "Here is my heart!"

EHRENFRIED LIEDICH.

DISCIPLINE.

"Zage nicht."

Tremble not, though darkly gather
    Clouds and tempest o'er thy sky;
Still believe, thy Heavenly Father
    Loves thee best when storms are nigh.

When the sun of fortune shineth
    Long and brightly on the heart,
Soon its fruitfulness declineth,
    Parched and dry in every part.

Then the plants of grace have faded
    In the dry and burning soil,
Thorns and briers their growth have shaded,
    Earthly cares and earthly toil.

But the clouds are seen ascending,
    Soon the heavens are overcast,
And the weary heart is bending
    'Neath affliction's stormy blast.

Yet the Lord, on high presiding,
   Rules the storm with powerful hand;
He the shower of grace is guiding
   To the dry and barren land.

See! at length the clouds are breaking,
   Tempests have not passed in vain;
For the soul, revived, awaking,
   Bears its fruits and flowers again.

Love divine has seen and counted
   Every tear it caused to fall,
And the storm which love appointed
   Was its choicest gift of all.
                    UNBEKANNTES.

JESUS, STILL LEAD ON.

"Jesu, geh voran."

Jesus, still lead on,
Till our rest be won!
And, although the way be cheerless,
We will follow, calm and fearless:
    Guide us by Thy hand
    To our Fatherland.

If the way be drear,
If the foe be near,
Let not faithless fears o'ertake us,
Let not faith and hope forsake us;
    For, through many a foe,
    To our home we go.

When we seek relief
From a long-felt grief,—
When oppressed by new temptations,
Lord, increase and perfect patience;

Show us that bright shore
Where we weep no more.

Jesus, still lead on,
Till our rest be won!
Heavenly Leader, still direct us,
Still support, console, protect us,
Till we safely stand
In our Fatherland!

LUDWIG VON ZINZENDORF.

TO A DYING CHILD.

"Zeuch-hin, mein Kind."

DEPART, my child! the Lord thy spirit calls
    To leave a world of woe.
Sad on my heart the heavenly summons falls;
    Yet since He wills it so,
I calm the rising agitation,
And say, with humble resignation,
            Depart, my child!

Depart, my child! lent for a little while
    Our drooping hearts to cheer;
Dear is thy loving voice, thy gentle smile
    Ah! who can tell how dear?
The sands are run—too quickly falling—
The Giver comes, His own recalling,—
            Depart, my child!

Depart, my child! enjoy in heaven's pure day
    What earth must still deny;—

TO A DYING CHILD.

Here many a storm awaits thy longer way,
    And many a tear thine eye.
Go, where the flowers have never faded,
Where love may smile unchilled, unshaded,—
        Depart, my child!

Depart, my child! soon shall we meet again
    In the good land of rest.
Thou goest, happy one! ere grief and pain
    Have reached thy gentle breast:
Happy, our thorny path forsaking,
From life's vain dream so early waking,—
        Depart, my child!

Depart, my child! angels are bending down
    To set thy spirit free;
The Saviour holds in heaven the golden crown
    He won on earth for thee.
Yes! now in Him thou art victorious,
Go, share His rest and triumph glorious,—
        Depart, my child!

              GOTTFRIED HOFFMANN.

ARISE!

"Wachet auf!"

Arise! ye lingering saints, arise!
    Remember that the night of grace,
When guilty slumbers sealed your eyes,
    Awakened you to run the race.
Now let not darkness round you fall,
But hearken to the Saviour's call—
                  Arise!

Arise! because the night of sin
    Must flee before the light of day;
God's glorious Gospel shining in
    Must chase the midnight gloom away:
You cannot true disciples be
If you still walk in vanity.
                    Arise!

Arise! although the flesh be weak,
    The spirit willing is and true,

And servants of the Master seek
  To follow where it guideth to.
Beloved! oh, be wise indeed,
And let the spirit ever lead.
                    Arise!

Arise! because our Serpent-foe
  Unwearied strives by day and night,
Remembers time is short below,
  And wrestles on with hellish might.
Then boldly grasp both sword and shield,—
Who slumbers on the battle-field?
                    Arise!

Arise! before that hour unknown,
  The hour of death, which comes ere long,
And comes not to the weak alone,
  But to the mighty and the strong.
Beloved! oft in spirit dwell
Upon the hour that none can tell.
                    Arise!

Arise! that you prepared may stand
  Before the coming of the Lord;
The day of wrath draws nigh at hand.
  According to th' eternal Word.

Ah! think, perhaps this day shall see
The dawning of eternity!
     Arise!

Arise! it is the Master's will;
 No more His heavenly voice despise:
Why linger with the dying still?
 He calls—Arouse you, and arise!
No longer slight the Saviour's call,
It sounds to you, to me, to all.
     Arise!
LUDWIG GOTTER.

GOD WITH ME.

"Gott bei mir an jedem Orte!"

My God with me in every place!
   Firmly does the promise stand,
On land or sea, with present grace
   Still to aid us near at hand.
   If you ask, "Who is with thee?"
   God is here—my God with me!

No depth, nor prison, nor the grave,
   Can exclude Him from His own;
His cheering presence still I have,
   If in crowds or all alone:
   In whatever state I be,
   Everywhere is God with me!

My God for me!—I dare to say,
   God the portion of my soul!
Nor need I tremble in dismay
   When around me troubles roll.

If you ask, " What comforts thee ? "
It is this—God is for me !

Ah ! faith has seen Him cradled lie
  Here on earth a weeping child;
Has seen Him for my vileness die,
  He, the sinless, undefiled !
And thus I know it true to be,
God, my Saviour, is for me !

In life, in death, with Him so near,
  Every battle I shall win ;
Shall boldly press through dangers here,
  Triumph over every sin !
" What ! shall *you* a victor be ? "
No, not I, but God in me !
C. H. ZELLER.

THE COMMUNION OF SAINTS.

"O wie selig seyd ihr doch, ihr Frommen!"

CHURCH ON EARTH.

"Oh how blessed are ye, saints forgiven,
  Through the gate of death now safe in heaven,
    All trials over,
  All the ills which round us darkly hover!"

CHURCH IN HEAVEN.

"Yes, dear friends, our joys are still increasing,
  Our songs of praise are new and never ceasing,
    All preparing
  For the time when you shall all be sharing."

CHURCH ON EARTH.

"We are now as in a prison dwelling,
  Storms of care and trouble o'er us swelling;
    All around us
  Only sins and griefs, to snare and wound us."

CHURCH IN HEAVEN.

"Ah, beloved friends! be not complaining;
Wish not joy while yet on earth remaining;
Be still confiding
In your Father's love and tender guiding."

CHURCH ON EARTH.

"In your quiet home so gently resting,
Safe for evermore from all molesting,
No care or sorrow
Can *you* feel to-day, or fear to-morrow!"

CHURCH IN HEAVEN.

"In your conflicts we were once engaging,
Long with sin and Satan warfare waging;
All your distresses
Once were ours, to weary and oppress us."

CHURCH ON EARTH.

"Christ has wiped away your every tear;
You enjoy what we are seeking here;
The harps of heaven
Sound in strains to mortals never given."

CHURCH IN HEAVEN.

"Yet in patience run the race before you;
Long for heaven, where Love is watching o'er you;

Sow in weeping,
Soon the fruit with joy you shall be reaping."

CHURCH ON EARTH.

" Come, come quickly, long-expected Jesus,
From all sin and sorrow to release us;
Quickly take us
To Thyself, and blest for ever make us!"

CHURCH IN HEAVEN.

" Ah, beloved souls! your palms victorious,
Golden harps, and thrones of triumph glorious,
All are waiting,—
Follow on with courage unabating."

CHORUS.

" Let us join to praise His name for ever,
To us both of every good the Giver;
Life undying
We shall each obtain, on Him relying.

" Praise Him, men on earth and saints in heaven!
To the Lamb be praise and glory given—
Praise unending,
Glory through eternity extending!"

SIMON DACH.

EVENING HYMN.

"Nun ruhen alle Wälder."

Quietly rest the woods and dales,
Silence round the hearth prevails,
    The world is all asleep;
Thou, my soul, in thought arise,
Seek thy Father in the skies,
And holy vigils with Him keep.

Sun, where hidest thou thy light?
Art thou driven hence by Night,
    Thy dark and ancient foe?
Go! another Sun is mine,
Jesus comes, with light divine,
To cheer my pilgrimage below.

Now that day has passed away,
Golden stars in bright array
    Bespangle the blue sky:
Bright and clear, so may I stand,
When I hear my Lord's command
To leave this earth, and upward fly.

EVENING HYMN.

Now this body seeks for rest,
From its vestments all undrest,
    Types of mortality:
Christ shall give me soon to wear,
Garments beautiful and fair,—
White robes of glorious majesty.

Head, and feet, and hands once more
Joy to think of labour o'er,
    And night with gladness see.
O my heart, thou too shalt know
Rest from all thy toil below,
And from earth's turmoil soon be free.

Weary limbs, now rest ye here,
Safe from danger and from fear,
    Seek slumber on this bed:
Deeper rest ere long to share,—
Other hands shall soon prepare
My narrow couch among the dead.

While my eyes I gently close,
Stealing o'er me soft repose,
    Who shall my guardian be?
Soul and body now I leave
(And Thou wilt the trust receive),
O Israel's Watchman! unto Thee.

EVENING HYMN.

O my friends, from you this day
May all ill have fled away,
    No danger near have come ;
Now, my God, these dear ones keep,
Give to my beloved sleep,
And angels send to guard their home !
PAUL GERHARD.

MY GOD! I KNOW THAT I MUST DIE.

"Mein Gott! ich weiss wohl dass ich sterbe."

My God! I know that I must die,
   My mortal life is passing hence;
On earth I neither hope nor try
   To find a lasting residence:
Then teach me, by Thy heavenly grace,
With joy and peace to end my race.

My God! I know not *when* I die,
   What is the moment, or the hour,
How soon the clay may broken lie,
   How quickly pass away the flower:
Then may Thy child preparëd be
Through time to meet Eternity.

My God! I know not *how* I die,
   For death has many ways to come—
In dark mysterious agony,
   Or gently as a sleep to some:

Just as Thou wilt! so I may be
For ever blessed, Lord, with Thee.

My God! I know not *where* I die,
   Where is my grave, beneath what strand;
Yet from its gloom I do rely
   To be delivered by Thy hand:
Content, I take what spot is mine,
Since all the earth, my Lord, is Thine.

My gracious God! when I must die,
   Oh, bear my happy soul above,
With Christ, my Lord, eternally
   To share Thy glory and Thy love!
Then comes it right and well to me,
When, where, and how my death shall be.

B. SCHMOLK.

LIGHT IN DARKNESS.

"Das Leben wird oft trübe."

How weary and how worthless this life at times appears!
What days of heavy musings, what hours of bitter tears!
How dark the storm-clouds gather along the wintry skies!
How desolate and cheerless the path before us lies!

And yet these days of dreariness are sent us from above;
They do not come in anger, but in faithfulness and love;
They come to teach us lessons which bright ones could not yield,
And to leave us blest and thankful when their purpose is fulfilled.

They come to draw us nearer to our Father and our Lord,
More earnestly to seek His face, to listen to His word,

And to feel, if now around us a desert land we see,
Without the star of promise, what would its darkness be!

They come to lay us lowly and humbled in the dust,
All self-deception swept away, all creature hope and trust;
Our helplessness, our vileness, our guiltiness to own,
And flee for hope and refuge to Christ, and Christ alone.

They come to break the fetters which here detain us fast,
And force our long-reluctant hearts to rise to heaven at last;
And brighten every prospect of that eternal home
Where grief and disappointment and fear can never come.

Then turn not in despondence, poor weary heart, away,
But meekly journey onwards through the dark and cloudy day:
Even now the bow of promise is above thee tinted bright,
And soon a joyful morning shall dissipate the night.

Thy God hath not forgot thee, and, when He sees it best,
Will lead thee into sunshine, will give thee bowers of rest;
And all thy pain and sorrow, when the pilgrimage is o'er,
Shall end in heavenly blessedness and joys for evermore!

SPITTA.

LET ME FIND THEE!

"Sieh, hier bin ich, Ehren-König."

BEHOLD me here, in grief draw near,
    Pleading at Thy throne, O King;
To Thee each tear, each trembling fear,
    Jesus, Son of man! I bring.
Let me find Thee,—let me find Thee,
    Me, a vile and worthless thing!

Look down in love, and from above
    With Thy Spirit satisfy;
Thou hast sought me, Thou hast bought me,
    And Thy purchase, Lord, am I.
Let me find Thee,—let me find Thee,
    Here on earth, and then on high!

No other prayer to Thee I bear,
    O my Lord, but only this,—
To share Thy grace, to see Thy face,
    And to know Thy people's bliss.

LET ME FIND THEE!

Let me find Thee,—let me find Thee,
  Thee to find is blessedness!

Hear the broken, scarcely spoken
  Utterance of my heart to Thee;
All the crying, all the sighing
  Of Thy child accepted be.
Let me find Thee,—let me find Thee,—
  Thus my soul longs vehemently!

Worldly pleasures, earthly treasures,
  Joys, and honours, will not stay;
They often pain, and, oh! how vain,
  As we pass from earth away!
Let me find Thee,—let me find Thee,
  Find Thee, O my God, this day!

JOACHIM NEANDER.

GRIEF AND CONSOLATION BY A MOTHER'S DEATH-BED.

"*Thatest sonst uns nicht zu Leide.*"

"Never couldst thou bear to grieve us,
Dearest mother,—why to-day?
Wherefore wilt thou thus forsake us,
Why, oh why, refuse to stay?"
"Were it but our Father's will,
Gladly had I tarried still."

"Mother, see the bursting anguish
Of thy dear ones, loved so well!
See our eyes with grief o'erflowing,
Grief which words refuse to tell!"
"Children, bid me not remain,
Let me see our Carl again!"

"Ah! and art thou really going
To that dark and distant shore?
All *our* cares, our joys, our sorrows,
All forgotten, shared no more!"

BY A MOTHER'S DEATH-BED.

"Children, think not, say not so,
  To the land of *love* I go."

"From the circle of affection,
  Mother, must *thou* next depart?
Ah! how many a link is broken
  Once uniting heart to heart!"
    "Closer draw that gentle chain
    Round the loved who yet remain."

"Canst thou then so gladly leave us?
  Is our grief unheeded now?
For thine eye is brightly beaming,
  Calm and cloudless is thy brow."
    "Yes! for faith, and hope, and love
    Draw me to my Lord above."

"Yet even there, in bliss undying,
  When thou numberest thine own,
Mother, shall not *we* be wanting,
  We, who here in bondage groan!"
    "Come, beloved! quickly come,
    Join me in our heavenly home!"

MÖWES.

AH! GRIEVE NOT SO.

"Nicht so traurig, nicht so sehr."

Ah! grieve not so, nor so lament,
    My soul! nor troubled sigh,
Because some joys to others sent
    Thy Father may deny;
Take all as love that seems severe—
There is no want if God is near.

There is no right thou canst demand,
    No title thou canst claim,
For all are strangers in the land
    Who bear the human name;
Earth and its treasures are the Lord's,
And He the lot of each accords.

How thankless art thou, child of man,
    For favours that abound!
Thy God has given thee eyes to scan
    The glory all around;

Yet seldom for this priceless sight,
Hast thou been heard to praise aright.

He knows, who lives on Zion's hill,
    What we in truth require,
Knows too how many blessings still
    This flesh and blood desire;
And could He safely all bestow,
He would not let thee sorrowing go.

Thou wert not born that earth should be
    A portion fondly sought;
Look up to heaven, and smiling see
    Thy shining, golden lot!
Honours and joys, which thou shalt share,
Unending and unenvied there!

Then journey on to life and bliss,
    God will protect to heaven;
And every good that meets thee is
    A blessing wisely given.
If losses come,—so let it be,
The God of heaven remains with thee!

PAUL GERHARD.

PILGRIM SONG.

"Kommt, Kinder, lasst uns gehen."

Come, brothers, let us onward,
    Night comes without delay,
And in this howling desert
    It is not good to stay.
    Take courage, and be strong!
We are hasting on to heaven,
Strength for warfare will be given,
    And glory won ere long.

The pilgrim's path of trial
    We do not fear to view;
We know His voice who calls us,
    The faithful One and true.
    Then, let who will contemn,
But, strong in His almighty grace,
Come, every one, with steadfast face,
    On to Jerusalem!

PILGRIM SONG.

If we would walk as pilgrims,
    We must not riches heap;
Much treasure to have gathered
    But makes the way more steep.
    We march with laggard speed,
Till every weight is cast aside,
Till with the little satisfied
    That pilgrimage can need.

Here, all unknown we wander,
    Despised on every hand,
Unnoticed, save when slighted
    As strangers in the land.
    Our joys they will not share,
Yet sing,—that they may catch the song
Of heaven, and the happy throng
    That now await us there!

Come, gladly, let us onward,
    Hand in hand still go,
Each helping one another
    Through all the way below.
    One family of love,—
Oh, let no voice of strife be heard,
No discord, by the angel-guard
    Who watch us from above.

PILGRIM SONG.

Soon, brothers, shall be ended
    The journey we've begun;
Endure a little longer,
    The race will soon be run.
  And in the land of rest,
In yonder bright, eternal home,
Where all the Father's loved ones come,
  We shall be safe and blest!

Then, boldly, let us venture,
    This, this is worth the cost!
Though dangers we encounter,
    Though everything is lost.
  O world! how vain thy call!
We follow Him who went before,
We follow to th' eternal shore,
  Jesus, our All in All!

GERHARD TERSTEEGEN.

MY FATHER IS THE MIGHTY LORD.

"Mein Vater ist der grosse Herr der Welt."

My Father is the mighty Lord, whose arm
Spans earth and sky, and shields His child from harm;
Whose still, small voice of love is yet the same
As once from Horeb's fiery mount it came;
Whose glorious works the angel-choirs declare:
He hears their praise,—and hearkens to my prayer.

My King is God's eternal, holy Son,
He who anoints me as a chosen one;
He has redeemed me with His precious blood,
And for unnumbered debts my surety stood;
He fought the foe, and drew me by His hand,
Out from his camp, into His Father's land.

My Brotherhood's a circle stretching wide
Around one fount, although a sea divide:
With fathers who behold the Lord in light,
With saints unborn who shall adore His might,

With brothers who the race of faith now run,
In union and communion, I am one!

My journey's end lies upward and afar,
It glimmers bright, but vaguely as a star,
And oft as faith has caught some glimpse serene,
So often clouds and mists obscure the scene;
Yet, in this longing ends each vision dim,
To see my Lord—and to be made like Him!

My grave, so long a dark and drear abyss,
Is now scarce noticed on the way to bliss:
Once at the gates of hell it yawning lay,
Now stands as portal to the land of day;
It takes me to the Father's home so blest,
It brings me to the feast, a welcome guest.

LANGE.

THY WILL BE DONE.

"Mein Jesu, wie du willt!"

My Jesus, as Thou wilt!
   Oh, may Thy will be mine!
Into Thy hand of love
   I would my all resign.
Through sorrow or through joy
   Conduct me as Thine own,
And help me still to say,
   My Lord, Thy will be done!

My Jesus, as Thou wilt!
   If needy here and poor,
Give me Thy people's bread,
   Their portion rich and sure.
The manna of Thy word
   Let my soul feed upon;
And if all else should fail—
   My Lord, Thy will be done!

THY WILL BE DONE.

My Jesus, as Thou wilt!
    If among thorns I go,
Still sometimes here and there
    Let a few roses blow.
But Thou on earth along
    The thorny path hast gone;
Then lead me after Thee,—
    My Lord, Thy will be done!

My Jesus, as Thou wilt!
    Though seen through many a tear.
Let not my star of hope
    Grow dim or disappear.
Since Thou on earth hast wept
    And sorrowed oft alone,
If I must weep with Thee,
    My Lord, Thy will be done!

My Jesus, as Thou wilt!
    If loved ones must depart,
Suffer not sorrow's flood
    To overwhelm my heart.
For they are blest with Thee,
    Their race and conflict won;
Let me but follow them—
    My Lord, Thy will be done!

THY WILL BE DONE.

My Jesus, as Thou wilt!
  When death itself draws nigh,
To Thy dear wounded side
  I would for refuge fly.
Leaning on Thee, to go
  Where Thou before hast gone;
The rest as Thou shalt please—
  My Lord, Thy will be done!

My Jesus, as Thou wilt!
  All shall be well for me,
Each changing future scene,
  I gladly trust with Thee.
Straight to my home above
  I travel calmly on,
And sing, in life or death,
  My Lord, Thy will be done!

B. SCHMOLK.

THE GOOD SHEPHERD.

"Ja führwahr! uns führt mit sanften Hand."

Yes! our Shepherd leads with gentle hand
 Through the dark pilgrim-land
 His flock, so dearly bought,
 So long and fondly sought.
    Hallelujah!

When in clouds and mist the weak ones stray,
 He shows again the way,
 And points to them afar
 A bright and guiding star.
    Hallelujah!

Tenderly He watches from on high
 With an unwearied eye;
 He comforts and sustains,
 In all their fears and pains.
    Hallelujah!

Through the parched, dreary desert He will guide
    To the green fountain-side;
    Through the dark, stormy night
    To a calm land of light.
              Hallelujah!

Yes! His "little flock" are ne'er forgot,
    His mercy changes not;
    Our home is safe above,
    Within His arms of love.
              Hallelujah!

KRUMMACHER.

REJOICE.

"Ermuntert euch, ihr Frommen."

Rejoice, all ye believers,
   And let your lights appear;
The evening is advancing,
   And darker night is near;
The Bridegroom is arising,
   And soon He draweth nigh,—
Up! pray, and watch, and wrestle,
   At midnight comes the cry!

See that your lamps are burning,
   Replenish them with oil,
And wait for your salvation,
   The end of earthly toil.
The watchers on the mountain
   Proclaim the Bridegroom near,
Go, meet Him as He cometh,
   With Hallelujahs clear!

REJOICE.

Ye wise and holy virgins,
    Now raise your voices higher,
Till in glad songs of triumph
    They meet the angel-choir.
The marriage-feast is waiting,
    The gates wide open stand;—
Arise! ye heirs of glory,
    The Bridegroom is at hand!

Ye saints, who here in patience
    Your cross and suff'rings bore,
Shall live and reign for ever
    When sorrow is no more;
Around the throne of glory,
    The Lamb ye shall behold,
In triumph cast before Him
    Your diadems of gold!

Palms of victory are there;
    There, radiant garments are;
There stands the peaceful harvest
    Beyond the reach of war;
There, after stormy winter,
    The flowers of earth arise,
And from the grave's long slumber
    Shall meet again our eyes!

REJOICE.

Our Hope and Expectation,
   O Jesus! now appear;
Arise, thou Sun, so longed for,
   O'er this benighted sphere!
With hearts and hands uplifted,
   We plead, O Lord, to see
The day of earth's redemption
   That brings us home to Thee!
LAURENTIUS LAURENTI.

THE ANGEL AND THE INFANT.

Smiling, a bright-eyed seraph bent
    Over an infant's dream,
To view his mirrored form he leant
    As in the crystal stream.

"Fair infant, come," he whispered low,
    "And leave the earth with me;
To a bright and happy land we'll go,
    This is no home for thee.

"Each sparkling pleasure knows alloy;
    Nor cloudless skies are here;
A care there is for every joy,
    For every smile a tear.

"The heart that dances free and light
    May soon be chained by sorrow;
The sun that sets in calm to-night
    May rise in storm to-morrow.

"Alas! to cloud a brow so fair,
  That griefs and pains should rise;
Alas! that this dark world of care
  Should dim these laughing eyes!

"To seek a brighter land with me,
  Infant, thou wilt not fear;
For piteous heaven the sad decree
  Recalls, that sent thee here."

It seemed on him the sweet babe smiled;
  His wings the seraph spread;
They're gone, the angel and the child,—
  Poor mother! thy son is dead!

UNBEKANNTES.

THE SERVICE OF THE LORD.

"O hochbeglückte Seele!"

How blessed, from the bonds of sin
    And earthly fetters free,
In singleness of heart and aim,
    Thy servant, Lord, to be!
The hardest toil to undertake
    With joy at Thy command,
The meanest office to receive
    With meekness at Thy hand.

With willing heart and longing eyes,
    To watch before Thy gate,
Ready to run the weary race,
    To bear the heavy weight;
No voice of thunder to expect,
    But follow calm and still,
For love can easily divine
    The One Beloved's will.

THE SERVICE OF THE LORD.

Thus may I serve Thee, gracious Lord!
    Thus ever Thine alone,
My soul and body given to Thee,
    The purchase Thou hast won.
Through evil or through good report
    Still keeping by Thy side,
And by my life or by my death
    Let Christ be magnified!

How happily the working days
    In this dear service fly;
How rapidly the closing hour,
    The time of rest draws nigh!
When all the faithful gather home,
    A joyful company,
And ever where the Master is,
    Shall His blest servants be.

                                Spitta.

THE DESIRED HAVEN.

"Lord, the waves are breaking o'er me and around,
  Oft of coming tempests I hear the moaning sound;
  Here there is no safety, rocks on either hand,
  'Tis a foreign roadstead, a strange and hostile land.
  Wherefore should I linger? others gone before
  Long since safe are landed on a calm and friendly shore.
  Now the sailing orders in mercy, Lord, bestow,—
             Slip the cable, let me go!

"Lord, the night is closing round my feeble bark,
  How shall I encounter its watches long and dark?
  Sorely worn and shattered by many a billow past,
  Can I stand another rude and stormy blast?
  Ah! the promised haven I never may attain,
  Sinking and forgotten amid the lonely main!
  Enemies around me, gloomy depths below,—
             Slip the cable, let me go!

"Lord, I would be near Thee, with Thee where Thou art,—
  Thine own Word hath said it, 'tis 'better to depart,'

There to serve Thee better, there to love Thee more,
With Thy ransomed people to worship and adore;
Ever to Thy presence Thou dost call Thine own,—
Why am I remaining, helpless and alone?
Now to see Thy glory, Thy wondrous love to know,—
     Slip the cable, let me go!

"Lord, the lights are gleaming from the distant shore
Where no billows threaten, where no tempests roar.
Long beloved voices calling me I hear,
Oh, how sweet *their* summons falls upon my ear!
Here are foes and strangers, faithless hearts and cold,
There is fond affection, fondly proved of old!
Let me haste to join them,—may it not be so?
     Slip the cable, let me go!"

Hark, the solemn answer!—hark, the promise sure!
"Blessed are the servants who to the end endure!
Yet a little longer hope and tarry on,
Yet a little longer, weak and weary one!
More to perfect patience, to grow in faith and love,
More *my* strength and wisdom and faithfulness to prove;
Then the sailing orders the Captain *shall* bestow,—
     Slip the cable, let thee go!"

         H. L. L.

THE LONG GOOD-NIGHT.

"Ich fahr dahin mit Freuden."

I JOURNEY forth rejoicing,
   From this dark vale of tears,
To heavenly joy and freedom,
   From earthly bonds and fears;
Where Christ our Lord shall gather
   All His redeemed again,
His kingdom to inherit,—
              Good-night, till then!

Go to thy quiet resting,
   Poor tenement of clay!
From all thy pain and weakness
   I gladly haste away;
But still in faith confiding
   To find thee yet again,
All glorious and immortal,—
              Good-night, till then!

Why thus so sadly weeping,
   Beloved ones of my heart?
The Lord is good and gracious,
   Though now He bids us part
Oft have we met in gladness,
   And we shall meet again,
All sorrow left behind us,—
            Good-night, till then!

I go to see His glory,
   Whom we have loved below;
I go, the blessed angels,
   The holy saints to know.
Our lovely ones departed,
   I go to find again,
And wait for you to join us,—
            Good-night, till then!

I hear the Saviour calling,
   The joyful hour has come,
The angel-guards are ready
   To guide me to our home;
Where Christ our Lord shall gather
   All His redeemed again,
His kingdom to inherit,—
            Good-night, till then!
                    UNBEKANNTES.

ALL THINGS ARE YOURS.

"Alles ist euer!"

ALL things are yours! O sweet message of mercy divine!
Christian brothers, rejoice in your portion and mine!
   Ours the high prize,
   Which poor sinners despise,
And for a vain world resign.

Raise your affections and heart to your home in the sky,
Then let the earth and its vanities wither and die;
   Your joys shall last,
   When theirs are long past,
Your treasure is laid up on high.

All things are yours, my beloved! our Lord from above
Watches His people with tender compassion and love.
   Hear His dear voice,—
   "My brethren, rejoice!
Nothing your safety shall move!"

All of things present that earth and her fulness can
    yield,
All of things future from knowledge and fancy con-
    cealed,
        Life's varied tale,
        Death's dark, dreaded vale,—
All as your portion revealed!

Heaven and earth, and the sea, and the systems of light,
Spirits unnumbered, angelic hosts holy and bright,
        All are for thee,
        Brother! be joyful with me,
Let us in praises unite!

Does thy heart sink in the conflict with fear and despair?
Are tears overflowing from fountains of sorrow and care?
        On yonder shore,
        See they are weeping no more,
Old things have passed away there!

Praise to the Saviour, whose death our salvation secures!
Praise to the Father, whose mercy for ever endures!
        New songs of praise
        Evermore let us raise,
Amen! yes, all things are yours!

                                SCHUBART.

THE WIDOW OF NAIN.

"O süsses Wort!"

Oh, sweetest words that Jesus could have sought
To soothe the mourning widow's heart, "Weep not!"
   They fall with comfort on my ear
   When life is dark and trouble near.

They were not whispered accents, but aloud
The Saviour spake them to the silent crowd,
   That each might hear His heavenly voice,
   And in the widow's joy rejoice!

Words that were spoken amid sorrow's strife,
And in the very midst of death and life,
   They shall refresh my soul at last,
   And strengthen me till life is past.

If poverty obscures my earthly lot,
Then shall I hear my Saviour say, "Weep not!"
   To God the Father raise thine eye,
   For still He hears the raven's cry.

And oh, should persecution's ruthless hand
Grant me no quiet possession in the land,
   The voice of Jesus calms each thought,
"Heaven is thy dwelling-place, Weep not!"

When dearest ones are called from earth away,
Christ can foretell a bright reunion-day:
"Weep not," He says, "poor mourning one,
   But think what I at Nain have done!"

When I myself am drawing near to death,
This Jesus shall be there, and thus He saith,
   "The race is run, the battle fought,
I am thy light, thy life, Weep not!"

Oh, sweetest words that Jesus could have sought
To cheer His weary troubled ones, "Weep not!"
   Thrice blessed words! I listening stay,
   Till grief and sorrow flee away!

DR. JOHANN HÖFEL.

CONFLICT.

"Schöne Sonne, kommst du endlich wieder?"

Sun of comfort, art thou fled for ever?
   Light of joy, wilt thou return at last?
Shall I sing again the song of morning,
   When the watches of the night are past?
Ah, delay not, long-expected dawning!
   Scatter the thick clouds and mist away
Which so dark on feeling and devotion,
   Over heart and memory, rest to-day!

Weeping I have stood alone in darkness,
   Gloomy cliffs above and depths below;
On the narrow pathway all forsaken,
   Left to wrestle with the accusing Foe;
Doubt and unbelief, and dark forebodings,
   Fearful spectres gathering around;—
Ah! my dizzy brain and foot were failing,
   Tottering over the abyss profound!

Yet One held me back! an arm almighty,
  Strong to save, as Satan to destroy!
From the giddy precipice He caught me,
  Drew me from despair to life and joy.
Jesus was my Helper! Saving mercy
  Is His work, His glory, His delight;
Many a chain of darkness He has broken,
  Changed to sunshine many a dismal night.

I will trust *again* His love, His power,
  Though I cannot *feel* His hand to-day;
To His help anew I will betake me,
  Though His countenance seem turned away!
Though without one smile, one gracious token,
  Through the flames and floods my path must go;
When the fires subside, the waves pass over,
  My Deliverer I again shall know.

Yes, the light of comfort shall return,
  Joy's sweet sun shall shine again at last;
I shall sing the gladsome song of morning,
  When the watches of the night are past;
It shall reappear, the welcome dawning,
  Scattering the clouds and mist away
Which so dark on feeling and devotion,
  Over heart and memory, rest to-day!

I shall find again the hopes long vanished,
    Like the swallows when the storms are gone;
Fountains shall be opened in the desert,
    Streams by the wayside, while journeying on.
Flowers of love and promise shall be springing
    Where the cruel thorn and wormwood sprung,
And the homeward path lie bright in sunshine
    Where my sad harp on the willows hung!

LANGE.

LOVE TO CHRIST.

"Ich will dich lieben."

I WILL love Thee, all my treasure!
   I will love Thee, all my strength!
I will love Thee, without measure,
   And will love Thee right at length.
Oh, I will love Thee, Light Divine,
Till I die and find Thee mine!

Alas! that I so lately knew Thee,
   Thee, so worthy of the best;
Nor had sooner turned to view Thee,
   Truest Good, and only Rest!
The more I love, I mourn the more
That I did not love before!

Far I ran, and wandered blindly,
   Seeking some created light;
Then I sought, but could not find Thee,
   I had wandered from Thee quite;
Until at last Thou wert made known
Through Thy seeking, not my own!

LOVE TO CHRIST.

I will praise Thee, Sun of Glory!
   Now Thy beams have gladness brought.
I will praise Thee, will adore Thee,
   For the light I vainly sought;
Will praise Thee that Thy words so blest
Spake my sin-sick soul to rest!

In Thy footsteps now uphold me,
   That I stumble not nor stray;
When the narrow way is told me,
   Never let me lingering stay:
But come, my weary soul to cheer,
Shine, eternal Sunbeam, here!

Be my heart more warmly glowing,
   Sweet and calm the tears I shed;
And its love, its ardour showing,
   Let my spirit onward tread.
Still, near to Thee, and nearer still,
Draw this heart, this mind, this will.

I will love, in joy and sorrow!
   Crowning joy! will love Thee well!
I will love, to-day, to-morrow,
   While I in this body dwell!
Oh! I will love Thee, Light Divine,
Till I die and find Thee mine!

                        JOHANN ANGELUS.

PARTING.

"Was macht ihr, dass ihr weinet."

WHAT mean ye by this wailing,
   To break my bleeding heart?
As if the love that binds us
   Could alter or depart!
Our sweet and holy union
   Knows neither time nor place;
The love that God has planted
   Is lasting as His grace.

Ye clasp these hands at parting,
   As if no hope could be,
While still we stand for ever
   In blessed unity!
Ye gaze, as on a vision
   Ye never could recall,
While still my heart is with you,
   And Jesus with us all!

PARTING.

Ye say, "We here, thou yonder;
    Thou goest, and we stay!"
And yet Christ's mystic body
    Is one eternally.
Ye speak of different journeys,
    A long and sad adieu,
While still one way I travel,
    And have one end with you!

Why should ye now be weeping
    These agonizing tears?
Behold our gracious Leader,
    And cast away your fears.
We tread *one* path to glory,
    Are guided by *one* hand,
And led in faith and patience
    Unto *one* Fatherland!

Then let this hour of parting
    No bitter grief record,
But be an hour of union
    More blessed with our Lord!
With Him to guide and save us,
    No changes that await,
No earthly separations,
    Can leave us desolate!

                      SPITTA.

THE ANGEL OF PATIENCE.

"Es zieht ein stiller Engel."

A GENTLE Angel walketh throughout a world of woe,
With messages of mercy to mourning hearts below;
His peaceful smile invites them to love and to confide,
Oh follow in His footsteps, keep closely by His side!

So gently will He lead thee through all the cloudy day,
And whisper of glad tidings to cheer the pilgrim way.
His courage never failing, when thine is almost gone,
He takes thy heavy burden, and helps to bear it on.

To soft and tearful sadness He changes dumb despair,
And soothes to deep submission the storm of grief and care;
Where midnight shades are brooding He pours the light of noon,
And every grievous wound He heals, most surely, if not soon.

He will not blame thy sorrows, while He brings the
    healing balm;
He does not chide thy longings, while He soothes them
    into calm;
And when thy heart is murmuring, and wildly asking,
    why?
He smiling beckons *forward*, points upward to the sky.

He will not always answer thy questions and thy fear;
His watchword is, "Be patient, the journey's end is
    near!"
And ever through the toilsome way, He tells of joys to
    come,
And points the pilgrim to his rest, the wanderer to his
    home.

SPITTA.

LOOKING HOME.

"Ach, uns wird das Herz so leer."

Ah! this heart is void and chill
    'Mid earth's noisy thronging,
For the Father's mansions still
    Vehemently is longing!

In the garments, once so strong,
    Now are rents distressing;
And the sandals, borne so long,
    Heavily are pressing.

Oh! to be at home, and gain
    All for which we're sighing,
From all earthly want and pain
    To be swiftly flying!

With this load of sin and care,
    Then, no longer bending;
But with waiting angels there,
    On our Lord attending!

Ah! how blessed, blessed they
  Who have rightly striven,
And rejoice eternally
  With their Lord in heaven!

SPITTA.

MORNING HYMN.

" Morgen-Glanz der Ewigkeit."

Jesus, Sun of Righteousness,
    Brightest beam of Love Divine,
With the early morning rays
    Do Thou on our darkness shine,
And dispel with purest light
All our night!

As on drooping herb and flower
    Falls the soft refreshing dew,
Let Thy Spirit's grace and power
    All our weary souls renew,
Showers of blessing over all
Softly fall!

Like the sun's reviving ray,
    May Thy love, with tender glow,
All our coldness melt away,
    Warm and cheer us forth to go,

MORNING HYMN.

Gladly serve Thee and obey
All the day!

O our only Hope and Guide,
  Never leave us, nor forsake;
Keep us ever at Thy side,
  Till the eternal morning break,
Moving on to Zion hill
Homeward still!

Lead us all our days and years
  In Thy straight and narrow way;
Lead us through the vale of tears
  To the land of perfect day,
Where Thy people, fully blest,
Safely rest!

K. VON ROSENMOTH.

RECALL.

"Kehre wieder, kehre wieder!"

RETURN, return!
Poor long-lost wanderer, home!
With all thy bitter tears,
Thy heavy burdens, come!
As thou art, all sin and pain,
Fear not to implore in vain.
See! the Father comes to meet thee,
Points to mercy's open door,
Words of life and promise greet thee,—
Ah, return, delay no more!

Return, return!
From strife and tumult vain
To quiet solitude,
To silent thought again.
There the storms shall sink to rest,
Which now desolate thy breast;

There the Spirit, long neglected,
   Waits with bliss before unknown,
And the Saviour, long rejected,
   Claims and seals thee for His own.

   Return, return!
From all thy crooked ways;
   Jesus will save the lost,
The fallen He can raise.
Look to Him who beckons thee
From the cross so lovingly;
See His gracious arms extended,
   Fear not to seek shelter there,
Where no grief is unbefriended,
   Where no sinner need despair.

   Return, return!
To thy long-suffering Lord;
   Fear not to seek His grace,
To trust His faithful word.
Yield to Him thy weary heart,
He can heal its keenest smart;
He can soothe the deepest sorrow,
   Wash the blackest guilt away:
Then delay not till to-morrow,
   Seek His offered gifts to-day.

RECALL.

Return, return!
From all thy wanderings, home!
From vanity and toil,
To rest and substance, come!
Come to Truth from Error's night,
Come from darkness unto light,
Come from death to life undying,
From a fallen earth to Heaven,—
Now the accepted time is flying,
Haste to take what God has given!

SPITTA.

GOING HOME.

"Unser Lieben sind gestorben."

Our beloved have departed,
While we tarry broken-hearted
  In the dreary, empty house;
They have ended life's brief story,
They have reached the home of glory,
  Over death victorious!

Hush that sobbing, weep more lightly;
On we travel, daily, nightly,
  To the rest that they have found,—
Are we not upon the river,
Sailing fast to meet for ever
  On more holy, happy ground?

Whilst with bitter tears we're mourning,
Thought to buried loves returning,
  Time is hasting us along,
Downward to the grave's dark dwelling,
Upward to the fountain welling
  With eternal life and song!

GOING HOME.

See ye not the breezes hieing?
Clouds along in hurry flying?
   But *we* haste more swiftly on,—
Ever changing our position,
Ever tossed in strange transition,—
   Here to-day, to-morrow gone!

Every hour that passes o'er us
Speaks of comfort yet before us,
   Of our journey's rapid rate,
And like passing vesper-bells,
The clock of time its chiming tells,
   At eternity's broad gate.

On we haste, to home invited,
There with friends to be united
   In a surer bond than here;
Meeting soon, and met for ever!
Glorious Hope! forsake us never,
   For Thy glimmering light is dear.

Ah, the way is shining clearer,
As we journey ever nearer
   To the everlasting home.
Friends, who there await our landing,
Comrades, round the throne now standing,
   We salute you, and we come!
                      LANGE.

THE JOURNEY TO JERUSALEM.

"Jesu, was hat dich getrieben?"

Jesus! what was that which drew Thee
    To Jerusalem's ancient gate?
Ah! the love that burned so truly
    Would not suffer Thee to wait!
On Thou journeyedst, thus securing
Me a city more enduring!

To my spirit, now, draw nearer,
    Lord! as to Jerusalem!
Let each moment prove Thee dearer,
    Make this heart a Bethlehem!
Thus my Saviour's love possessing,
Surely I have Salem's blessing.

To the world Thou hast sent me,
    Like the twelve that saw Thy face;
Lead me through the journey gently,
    Keep me near Thee by Thy grace,
My allotted work fulfilling,
Ever ready, ever willing.

Let me gladly see my calling,
    When and where Thou sendest me,
Never into darkness falling,
    Gazing on futurity;
But obey when Thou hast bidden,
Though Thy counsel should be hidden.

Let me follow Thee, my Saviour,
    Not with words or empty show;
Let my heart, my life, behaviour,
    Prove Thy presence here below.
Meekly with the froward bearing,
And each brother's burden sharing!

O my Lord! if Thou shouldst ever
    Call me desolate to roam,
For Thy truth and conscience sever
    Every tie of house and home,—
Robbed of every other blessing,
I am rich, Thy love possessing!

So shall I, hosannahs singing,
    All the desert-way rejoice;
Late and early, praises bringing,
    Though with often faltering voice,—
Yet my feeble notes ascending,
With the strains of heaven are blending!

LAURENTIUS LAURENTI.

THE MERCHANT.

"Einen Kaufmann sieht man ohne Gleichen."

Once a merchant travelled far and wide,
Over mountain-chains and ocean's tide;
Slighted and despised on every hand,
Wearily he passed from land to land.

Not with treasure treasures to acquire,
Seemed the wanderer's purpose or desire;
Gold and silver he regarded not,—
Pearls alone with eagerness he sought.

Many were produced to meet his call;—
Strictly he examined, weighed them all;
Nothing could deceive, or please his eye,
Calmly he surveyed, and passed them by.

Sadly he pursued his search around,—
Ah! the *One* 'midst many was not found!
Stars indeed he saw, but not the Sun
All his longings sought and dwelt upon.

Weary now with all his wanderings vain,
To his native home he turns again.
There he finds a Fisher on the strand,
Stooping down to draw a net to land.

What new treasures of the deep are these?
Who this unknown Stranger of the seas?
Changed his aspect now, his bearing high,
While he speaks with gentle dignity :—

" Peace be with thee ! Now thou mayest obtain
All so long desired and sought in vain,—
Thou 'mid many fools the only wise,
At thy journey's end behold the prize !"

" Yes, it is the One, beyond compare,
Sought so long, abandoned in despair.
Stranger, speak, how may it be my own ?"
" *All thou hast* can be the price alone."

" Be it so !" he joyfully replied ;
" Lord, take all, and take myself beside !
For in wondrous love Thou bring'st from heaven
What no monarch has or could have given."

And the world deceived and foolish call
Him, who for one jewel gave his all;

But unheeding what they think or say,
Glad and satisfied he goes his way.

Food is his which they have never known,
Cordials granted to himself alone;
From earth's vanities and cares set free,
Now he walks in peace and liberty.

Wondrous blessings reach him from above,
Love comes down to meet the heart of love;
Ever as he views his treasure bright,
All his soul is filled with life and light.

Blessed they who find the priceless gem,
Blessed they who seek! It shines for them
Brightly still, the prize by God revealed
For the victor on Faith's battle-field.
From the Kirchen-Freund.

SUBMISSION.

"Stille, mein Wille! dein Jesu hilft siegen."

Be still, my soul!—the Lord is on thy side,
 Bear patiently the cross of grief or pain;
Leave to thy God to order and provide,
 In every change He faithful will remain.
Be still, my soul!—thy best, thy Heavenly Friend
Through thorny ways leads to a joyful end.

Be still, my soul!—thy God doth undertake
 To guide the future, as He has the past:
Thy hope, thy confidence, let nothing shake,
 All now mysterious shall be bright at last.
Be still, my soul!—the waves and winds still know
His voice, who ruled them while He dwelt below.

Be still, my soul!—when dearest friends depart,
 And all is darkened in the vale of tears,
Then shalt thou better know His love, His heart,
 Who comes to soothe thy sorrow and thy fears.
Be still, my soul!—thy Jesus can repay
From His own fulness all He takes away.

Be still, my soul!—the hour is hastening on
   When we shall be for ever with the Lord;
When disappointment, grief, and fear are gone,
   Sorrow forgot, Love's purest joys restored.
Be still, my soul!—when change and tears are past,
All safe and blessed we shall meet at last.

Be still, my soul!—begin the song of praise
   On earth, believing, to thy Lord on high;
Acknowledge Him in all thy works and ways,
   So shall He view thee with a well-pleased eye.
Be still, my soul!—the Sun of life divine
Through passing clouds shall but more brightly shine.

UNBEKANNTES.

WAITING.

"Meine Stunde ist noch nicht kommen"

"Jesus' hour is not yet come;"—
    Let this word thine answer be.
Pilgrim, asking for thy home,
    Longing to be blest and free.
Yet a season tarry on—
Nobly borne, is nobly done.

While oppressing cares and fears
    Night and day no respite leave,
Still prolonged through many years,
    None to help thee or relieve;
Hold the word of promise fast,
Till deliverance comes at last.

Every creature-hope and trust,
    Every earthly prop or stay,
May lie prostrate in the dust,
    May have failed or passed away;—

Then, when darkest falls the night,
Jesus comes, and all is light.

Yes, the Comforter draws nigh
   To the breaking, bursting heart,
For, with tender sympathy,
   He has seen and felt its smart:
Through its darkest hours of ill,
He is waiting, watching still.

Dost thou ask, *When* comes His hour?
   Then, when it shall aid thee best.
Trust His faithfulness and power,
   Trust in Him, and quietly rest.
Suffer on, and hope, and wait,—
Jesus never comes too late.

Blessed day, which hastens fast,
   End of conflict and of sin!
Death itself shall die at last,
   Heaven's eternal joys begin.
Then eternity shall prove,
God is Light, and God is Love.

SPITTA.

PRAISE AND PRAYER.

"O treuer Heiland Jesu Christ."

We praise and bless Thee, gracious Lord,
    Our Saviour kind and true,
For all the old things passed away,
    For all Thou hast made new.

The old security is gone,
    In which so long we lay;
The sleep of death Thou hast dispelled,
    The darkness rolled away.

New hopes, new purposes, desires,
    And joys, Thy grace has given;
Old ties are broken from the earth,
    New ones attach to heaven.

But yet how much must be destroyed,
    How much renewed must be,

Ere we can fully stand complete
  In likeness, Lord, to Thee!

Ere to Jerusalem above,
  The holy place, we come,
Where nothing sinful or defiled
  Shall ever find a home!

Thou, only Thou, must carry on
  The work Thou hast begun;
Of Thine own strength Thou must impart,
  In Thine own ways to run.

Ah, leave us not! from day to day
  Revive, restore again;
Our feeble steps do Thou direct,
  Our enemies restrain.

Whate'er would tempt the soul to stray,
  Or separate from Thee,
That, Lord, remove, however dear
  To the poor heart it be!

When the flesh sinks, then strengthen Thou
  The spirit from above;
Make us to feel Thy service sweet,
  And light Thy yoke of love.

So shall we faultless stand at last
　　Before Thy Father's throne,
The blessedness for ever ours,
　　The glory all Thine own!

SPITTA.

CALVARY.

"Fliesst, ihr Augen, fliesst von Thränen."

Flow, my tears, flow on still faster,
   Thus my guilt and sin bemoan;
Mourn, my heart, in deeper anguish,
   Over sorrows not thine own!
   See, a spotless Lamb draw nigh
   To Jerusalem, to die
   For thy sins, the sinless One;—
   Think! ah, think! what thou hast done!

See Him stand, while cruel fetters
   Bind the hands that framed the world,
While around Him bitter mocking,
   Laughter, and contempt are hurled.
   Heathen rage and Jewish scorn,
   Meekly for our sins are borne.
   Sin has brought Him from above;
   Who can fathom such a love?

CALVARY.

Soon the heavy doom is spoken,
 Even Pilate's pleading ceased;
Jesus to the cross is chosen,
 And Barabbas is released!
 Ah! there is no loving word,
 Not one voice of pity heard,
 But the loud and frenzied cry,
"Crucify Him,—crucify!"

Can we view the Saviour given
 To the smiter's hands for us?
Can we all unmoved, unhumbled,
 See Him mocked and slighted thus,—
 View the thorny chaplet made
 For His meek and silent head,—
 Hear the loud and angry din,
 And not tremble for our sin?

Follow from the hall of judgment
 This sad Saviour on His way;
But, in spirit, on the journey,
 Often pause, and humbly pray;—
 Pray the Father to behold
 By the Son thy ransom told,
 And a substitute for thee
 In His Well-beloved see!

CALVARY.

Must I, Jesus, thus behold Thee
  In Thy toil and sorrow here?
Can I nothing better yield Thee
  Than my unavailing tear?
  Lamb of God! I weep for Thee!
  Weep, Thy cruel cross to see,—
  Weep, for death that death destroys!
  Weep, for grief that brings me joys!

Poor is all that I can offer,
  Soul and body while I live;
Take them, O my Saviour, take them,
  I have nothing more to give.
  Come, and in this heart remain,
  Let each enemy be slain,—
  Let me live and die with Thee;
  To Thy kingdom welcome me!

Loud and louder, saints are singing,
  Glory! glory! Christ, to Thee!
Over death and hell for ever
  Thou hast triumphed gloriously.
  I am Thine, and Thou art mine:
  Oh! to see Thy brightness shine!
  Lord! Thy day of grief is o'er,
  Come! in glory,—come once more!
LAURENTIUS LAURENTI.

RE-UNION.

" Wiedersehn! ja, wiedersehn wird einst."

MEET again! yes, we shall meet again,
Though now we part in pain!
    His people all
      Together Christ shall call.
                Hallelujah!

Soon the days of absence shall be o'er,
And thou shalt weep no more;
    Our meeting day
      Shall wipe all tears away.
                Hallelujah!

Now I go with gladness to our home,
With gladness thou shalt come;
    There I will wait
      To meet thee at Heaven's gate.
                Hallelujah!

RE-UNION.

Dearest! what delight, again to share
Our sweet communion there,
    In bliss among
    The holy ransomed throng!
        Hallelujah!

Here, in many a grief our hearts were one,
There, shall be joys alone;
    Joy fading never,
    Increasing, deepening ever.
        Hallelujah!

Not to mortal sight can it be given
To know the bliss of Heaven;
    But thou shalt be
    Soon there, and sing with me,
        Hallelujah!

Meet again! yes, we shall meet again,
Though now we part in pain!
    Together all
    His people Christ shall call.
        Hallelujah!

M. A. ZILLE.

JESUS ALL-SUFFICIENT.

"*Wenn ich ihn nur habe.*"

If only He is mine,—
    If but this poor heart
  Never more, in grief or joy,
    May from Him depart,
Then farewell to sadness;
All I feel is love, and hope, and gladness.

  If only He is mine,—
    Then, from all below,
  Leaning on my pilgrim-staff,
    Gladly forth I go,
From the crowd who follow
In the broad, bright road, their pleasures false
    and hollow.

    If only He is mine,—
      Then all else is given;

JESUS ALL-SUFFICIENT.

    Every blessing lifts my eyes
        And my heart to Heaven.
Filled with heavenly love,
Earthly hopes and fears no longer tempt or move.

    There,—where He is mine,
        Is my Fatherland,
    And my heritage of bliss
        Daily cometh from His hand.
Now I find again
In His people love long lost, and mourned in vain.
NOVALIS.

ANTICIPATION.

" Wie wird mir seyn?"

What shall I be, my Lord, when I behold Thee
   In awful majesty at God's right hand,
And 'mid th' eternal glories that enfold me,
   In strange bewilderment, O Lord, I stand?
What shall I be? These tears,—they dim my sight,
I cannot catch the blissful vision right.

What shall I be, Lord, when Thy radiant glory,
   As from the grave I rise, encircles me;
When brightly pictured in the light before me,
   What eye hath never seen, my eyes shall see?
What shall I be? Ah, blessed and sublime
Even the dim prospect of that glorious time!

What shall I be, when days of grief are ended,
   From earthly fetters set for ever free;
When from the harps of saints and angels blended,
   I hear the burst of joyful melody?

ANTICIPATION.

What shall I be, when, risen from the dead,
Sin, death, and hell I never more shall dread?

What shall I be, when all around are thronging,
    The loved of earth, where I have come to dwell;
When all is joy and praise,—no anxious longing,
    No bitter parting, and no sad farewell?
What shall I be? Ah, how the streaming light
Can lend a radiance to this dreary night!

Yes! faith can never know the full salvation
    Which Jesus for His people will prepare:
Then will I wait in peaceful expectation,
    Till the Good Shepherd comes to take me there.
My Lord, my God, a blissful end I see,
Though now I know not what I yet shall be!

LANGBECKER.

"GOD CALLING YET."

"Gott rufet noch!"

God calling yet!—and shall I never hearken,
But still earth's witcheries my spirit darken?
This passing life, these passing joys, all flying,
And still my soul in dreamy slumbers lying!

God calling yet!—and I not yet arising,
So long His loving, faithful voice despising,
So coldly His unwearied care repaying,—
He calls me still, and still I am delaying!

God calling yet!—loud at my door is knocking,
And I my heart, my ear, still firmer locking:
He still is ready, willing to receive me,
Is waiting now, but ah! He soon may leave me.

God calling yet!—and I no answer giving;
I dread His yoke, and am in bondage living;
Too long I linger, but not yet forsaken,
He calls me still, O my poor heart, awaken!

"GOD CALLING YET."

Ah, yield Him all,—all to His care confiding;
Where but with Him are rest and peace abiding?
Unloose, unloose, break earthly bonds asunder,
And let this spirit rise in soaring wonder.

God calling yet!—I can no longer tarry,
Nor to my God a heart divided carry;
Now, vain and giddy world, your spells are broken!
Sweeter than all, the voice of God has spoken!

GERHARD TERSTEEGEN.

RESIGNATION.

"Ich hab' in guten Stunden."

I have had my days of blessing,
All the joys of life possessing,—
   Unnumbered they appear!
Then, let faith and patience cheer me,
Now that trials gather near me;
   Where is life without a tear?

Yes, O Lord, a sinner looking
O'er the sins Thou art rebuking,
   Must own Thy judgments light.
Surely, I so oft offending,
Shall, in humble patience bending,
   Feel Thy chastisements are right.

Let me, o'er transgression weeping,
Find the grace my soul is seeking;
   Receiving at Thy throne

Strength to meet each tribulation,
Looking for the great salvation,
    Trusting in my Lord alone!

While though oft with tears and sighing,
Still to praise Thee feebly trying,
    Still clinging, Lord, to Thee;
Quietly on Thy love relying,
I am Thine,—and living, dying,
    Surely all is well with me!

CHRISTIAN GELLERT.

REST.

"Ich bleib bei dir!"

I REST with Thee, Lord! whither should I go?
    I feel so blest within Thy home of love!
The blessings purchased by Thy pain and woe,
    To Thy poor child Thou sendest from above.
Oh never let Thy grace depart from me,
So shall I still abide, my Lord, with Thee.

I rest with Thee! Eternal life the prize
    Thou wilt bestow, when faith's good fight is won.
What can earth give, but vain regrets and sighs,
    To the poor heart whose passing bliss is done?
For lasting joys I fleeting ones resign,
Since Jesus calls me His, and He is mine.

I rest with Thee! no other place of rest
    Can now attract, no other portion please:
The soul, of heavenly treasure now possest,
    All earthly glory with indifference sees.

Poor world, farewell! thy splendours tempt no more,
The power of grace I feel, and thine is o'er.

I rest with Thee! with Thee, whose wondrous love
    Descends to seek the lost, the fallen raise.
Oh that my whole of future life might prove
    One hallelujah, one glad song of praise!
So shall I sing, as time's last moments flee,
Now and for ever, Lord, I rest with Thee!

ADOLPH MORAHT.

LOOKING TO JESUS.

"O stilles Lamm."

O SILENT Lamb! for me Thou hast endured,
   Jesus, Thou holy, perfect, sinless One!
Thy grief and bitter anguish have secured
   My soul's salvation, when this race is run.
     Then let me, to Thine image true,
Thus meekly suffer, with the crown in view.

The narrow way which leads us up to Heaven
   Must here through strife and tribulation lie;
Then, on the thorny path may strength be given,
   This sinful flesh, O Lord, to crucify.
     Oh, take this feebleness away,
And make me strong to meet each future day!

Here, daily crosses come to try our weakness,
   Here, every member must a burden bear;
But, O my Saviour, if I take with meekness
   The cross appointed by Thy love and care,

Too great, too long, it will not be,
For it is weighed and measured out by Thee.

If thus we journey patiently through sadness,
    Each grief will make us dearer to our Lord;
But if we flee the cross, in search of gladness,
    We cannot shun His dread, avenging sword.
    Oh, blessed they who hear the call,
Who take the cross, and follow, leaving all!

So help me, Lord, Thy holy will to suffer,
    And still a learner at Thy feet to be;
Give faith and patience when the way is rougher,
    And at the end a joyful victory.
    Thus grief itself is changed to song,
Ofttimes on earth, but evermore ere long.
KARL HEINRICH VON BOGATZKI.

PRAISE.

"Lobe den Herren!"

PRAISE to Jehovah, the almighty King of Creation!
Swell Heaven's chorus, chime in every heart, every nation!
   O my soul, wake!
  Harp, lute, and psaltery take,
Sound forth in glad adoration!

Praise to Jehovah! whose love o'er thy course is attending,
Redeeming thy life, and thee from all evil defending.
   Through all the past,
  O my soul, over thee cast,
His sheltering wings were bending!

Praise to Jehovah! whose fence has been planted around thee,
Who, from His heavens, with blessing and mercy has crowned thee.

Think, happy one!
What He can do, and has done,
Since in His pity He found thee.

Praise to Jehovah! all that has breath praise Him,
  sing praises;
Bless God, O my soul, and all that is in me, sing praises!
  In Him rejoice,
    Until for ever thy voice
The hymn of eternity raises!

JOACHIM NEANDER.

HYMN SUNG AT A FUNERAL

"Wohlauf! wohlan! zum letzten Gang."

Come forth! come on, with solemn song!
The road is short, the rest is long!
The Lord brought here, He calls away,
    Make no delay,—
This home was for a passing day.

Here in an inn a stranger dwelt,
Here joy and grief by turns he felt:
Poor dwelling, now we close thy door!
    The task is o'er,
The sojourner returns no more!

Now of a lasting home possest,
He goes to seek a deeper rest.
Good night! the day was sultry here,
    In toil and fear,
Good night! the night is cool and clear.

HYMN SUNG AT A FUNERAL.

Chime on, ye bells! again begin,
And ring the Sabbath morning in;
The labourer's week-day work is done,
      The rest begun,
Which Christ hath for His people won!

Now open to us, gates of peace!
Here let the pilgrim's journey cease.
Ye quiet slumberers, make room
      In your still home
For the new stranger who has come!

How many graves around us lie!
How many homes are in the sky!
Yes, for each saint doth Christ prepare
      A place with care;—
Thy home is waiting, brother, there!

Jesus, Thou reignest, Lord alone!
Thou wilt return and claim Thine own.
Come quickly, Lord! return again!
      Amen! Amen!
Thine seal us ever, now and then!

                        F. SACHSE.

RESURRECTION.

"Auferstehn, ja, auferstehn wirst du."

Thou shalt rise! my dust, thou shalt arise!
Not always closed thine eyes;
    Thy life's first Giver
    Will give thee life for ever,—
        Ah, praise His name!

Sown in darkness, but to bloom again,
When, after winter's reign,
    Jesus is reaping
    The seed now quietly sleeping,—
        Ah, praise His name!

Day of praise! for thee, thou wondrous day,
In my quiet grave I stay;
    And when I number
    My days and nights of slumber,
        Christ waketh me!

Then, as they who dream, we shall arise
With Jesus to the skies,
    And find, that morrow,
    The weary pilgrim's sorrow
        All past and gone!

Then, within the Holiest, I shall tread,
By my Redeemer led,
    Through Heaven soaring,
    His holy name adoring
        Eternally!

          KLOPSTOCK.

HERE AND THERE.

"Was kein Auge hat gesehen."

What no human eye hath seen,
   What no mortal ear hath heard,
What on thought hath never been
   In its noblest flights conferred,—
This hath God prepared in store
For His people evermore!

When the shaded pilgrim land
   Fades before my closing eye,
Then revealed on either hand,
   Heaven's own scenery shall lie:
Then the veil of flesh shall fall,
Now concealing, darkening all.

Heavenly landscapes, calmly bright,
   Life's pure river murmuring low,
Forms of loveliness and light,
   Lost to earth long time ago,—

Yes, mine own, lamented long,
Shine amid the angel throng!

Many a joyful sight was given,
   Many a lovely vision here,
Hill, and vale, and starry even,
   Friendship's smile, Affection's tear:
These were shadows, sent in love,
Of realities above!

When upon my wearied ear
   Earth's last echoes faintly die,
Then shall angel harps draw near,
   All the chorus of the sky;
Long-hushed voices blend again,
Sweetly, in that welcome-strain.

Here were sweet and varied tones,
   Bird, and breeze, and fountain's fall;
Yet Creation's travail-groans
   Ever sadly sighed through all.
There no discord jars the air,
Harmony is perfect there!

When this aching heart shall rest,
   All its busy pulses o'er,

From her mortal robes undrest
  Shall my spirit upward soar.
Then shall unimagined joy
All my thoughts and powers employ.

Here devotion's healing balm
  Often came to soothe my breast,
Hours of deep and holy calm,
  Earnests of eternal rest;
But the bliss was here unknown,
Which shall there be all my own!

Jesus reigns, the Life, the Sun,
  Of that wondrous world above;
All the clouds and storms are gone,
  All is light, and all is love;
All the shadows melt away
In the blaze of perfect day!

LANGE.

JOY IN BELIEVING.

"Ich glaube, Hallelujah!"

Hallelujah! I believe!
  Now the giddy world stands fast;
Now my soul has found an anchor
  Till the night of storm is past.
All the gloomy mists are rising,
  And a clue is in my hand,
Through earth's labyrinth to guide me
  To a bright and heavenly land.

Hallelujah! I believe!
  Sorrow's bitterness is o'er,
And affliction's heavy burden
  Weighs my spirit down no more.
On the cross the mystic writing
  Now revealed before me lies,
While I read the words of comfort,
  "As a father, I chastise."

JOY IN BELIEVING.

Hallelujah! I believe!
　Now no longer on my soul
All the debt of sin is lying,—
　One great Friend has paid the whole!
Ice-bound fields of legal labour
　I have left, with all their toil;
While the fruits of love are growing
　From a new and genial soil.

Hallelujah! I believe!
　Now life's mystery is gone,
Gladly through its fleeting shadows,
　To the end I journey on.
Through the tempest, or the sunshine,—
　Over flowers or ruins led,
Still the path is *homeward* hasting,
　Where all sorrow shall have fled.

Hallelujah! I believe!
　Now, O Love, I know thy power,
Thine no false or fragile fetters,
　Not the rose-wreaths of an hour!
Christian bonds of holy union,
　Death itself does not destroy;
Yes, to live, and love for ever,
　Is our heritage of joy!

MÖWES.

LOWLY.

"Hinab geht Christi Weg."

CHRIST's path was sad and lowly,
  But yet thou, in thy pride,
Wouldst climb the highest summit,
  And on the height abide!
Wouldst thou to heaven arise?
  Thy Lord the way will show thee;
For who would climb these skies,
  Must first with Him be lowly.

Lowly, my soul, be lowly,—
  Follow the paths of old:
The feather riseth lightly,
  But never so the gold!
The stream, descending fast,
  Has gathered, quietly, slowly,—
A river rolls at last,—
  Therefore, my soul, be lowly.

LOWLY.

Lowly, my eyes, be lowly:
    God, from His throne above,
Looks down upon the humble
    In kindness and in love.
Still, as I rise, I shall
    Have greater depths below me,
And haughty looks must fall,—
    Therefore, mine eyes, be lowly

Lowly, my hands, be lowly:
    Christ's poor around us dwell,
Stoop down, and kindly cherish
    The flock He loves so well.
Not toiling to secure
    This world's fame and glory,—
Thy Saviour blessed the poor,
    Therefore, my hands, be lowly.

Lowly, my heart, be lowly:
    So God shall dwell with thee;
It is the meek and patient
    Who shall exalted be.
Deep in the valley rest
    The Spirit's gifts most holy,
And they who seek are blest,—
    Therefore, my heart, be lowly.

LOWLY.

Lowly, I would be lowly!
  This frame, to earth allied,
Must first to dust be humbled
  Ere it be glorified!
My God, prepare me here
  For all that lies before me;
I would in heaven appear,
  And so I would be lowly.

INGOLSTELLER.

THE CHRISTIAN CROSS.

"Der Christen Schmuck und Ordensband."

The Christian's badge of honour here,
   Has ever been the cross;
And when its hidden joys appear,
   He counts it gain, not loss.

He bears it meekly, as is best,
   While struggling here with sin;
He wears it not upon his breast—
   Ah! no, it is within.

And if it bring him pain or shame,
   He takes it joyfully;
For well he knows from whom it came,
   And what its end shall be.

Only a little while 'tis borne,
   And as a pledge is given,
Of robes of triumph, to be worn
   For evermore in heaven.

SPITTA.

SONG OF THE SOJOURNER.

"Ich bin ein Gast auf Erden."

A PILGRIM and a stranger,
  I journey here below;
Far distant is my country,
  The home to which I go.
Here I must toil and travel,
  Oft weary and opprest;
But there my God shall lead me
  To everlasting rest.

I've met with storms and danger,
  Even from my early years,
With enemies and conflicts,
  With fightings and with fears.
There's nothing here that tempts me
  To wish a longer stay,
So I must hasten forwards,—
  No halting or delay.

SONG OF THE SOJOURNER.

It is a well-worn pathway,—
   Many have gone before:
The holy saints and prophets,
   The patriarchs of yore.
They trod the toilsome journey
   In patience and in faith;
And them I fain would follow,
   Like them in life and death!

Who would share Abraham's blessing
   Must Abraham's path pursue,
A stranger and a pilgrim,
   Like him, must journey through.
The foes must be encountered,
   The dangers must be passed;
Only a faithful soldier
   Receives the crown at last.

So I must hasten forwards,—
   Thank God, the end will come!
This land of my sojourning
   Is not my destined home.
That evermore abideth,
   Jerusalem above,
The everlasting city,
   The land of light and love.

There still my thoughts are dwelling;
   'Tis there I long to be!
Come, Lord, and call Thy servant
   To blessedness with Thee!
Come, bid my toils be ended,
   Let all my wanderings cease;
Call from the wayside lodging,
   To the sweet home of peace!

There I shall dwell for ever,
   No more a stranger guest,
With all Thy blood-bought children
   In everlasting rest;
The pilgrim toils forgotten,
   The pilgrim conflicts o'er,
All earthly griefs behind us,
   Eternal joys before!

PAUL GERHARDT.

THE CHRISTIAN HOUSEHOLD.

"O selig Haus!"

O HAPPY HOUSE! where Thou art loved the best,
   Dear Friend and Saviour of our race,
Where never comes such welcomed honoured
      Guest,
   Where none can ever fill Thy place:
Where every heart goes forth to meet Thee,
   Where every ear attends Thy word,
Where every lip with blessing greets Thee,
   Where all are waiting on their Lord.

O happy house! where two are one in heart,
   In holy faith and hope are one,
Whom death can only for a little part,
   Not end the union here begun:
Who share together one salvation,
   Who would be with Thee, Lord, always,
In gladness, or in tribulation,
   In happy or in evil days.

O happy house! whose little ones are given
  Early to Thee, in faith and prayer,—
To Thee, their Friend, who from the heights of heaven
  Guards them with more than mother's care.
O happy house! where little voices
  Their glad hosannahs love to raise,
And childhood's lisping tongue rejoices
  To bring new songs of love and praise.

O happy house! and happy servitude!
  Where all alike one Master own;
Where daily duty, in Thy strength pursued,
  Is never hard nor toilsome known;
Where each one serves Thee, meek and lowly,
  Whatever Thine appointment be,
Till common tasks seem great and holy,
  When they are done as unto Thee.

O happy house! where Thou art not forgot
  When joy is flowing full and free;
O happy house! where every wound is brought,
  Physician, Comforter, to Thee.
Until at last, earth's day's-work ended,
  All meet Thee in that home above,
From whence Thou camest, where Thou hast ascended,
  Thy heaven of glory and of love!

SPITTA.

THE TWO JOURNEYS.

"Wohin, wohin?"

"WHITHER, oh, whither?"—"With blindfolded eyes,
  Down a wild torrent under stormy skies,
  A gulf between two dark eternities,
        Drifting, we know not where!"

"Whither, oh, whither?"—"To a land of light,
  A home of loveliness serene and bright,
  Joyfully hastening, with steady flight,
        Our hearts before us there!"

"Whither, oh, whither?"—"Life's short pleasures past,
  Hope's funeral knell the sound on every blast,
  Heaven's entrance closed, to ruin hurried fast,
        A leaf before the wind!"

"Whither, oh, whither?"—"Pilgrims near their home,
  No longer in a foreign land to roam;
  Bright and beloved ones waiting till we come—
        All sorrow left behind!"

THE TWO JOURNEYS.

"Whither, oh, whither?"—"Who the path can say
  To where some star will lend a cheering ray?
  Or through earth's labyrinth direct our way,
          So wildly sought in vain!"

"Whither, oh, whither?"—"Christ the risen One,
  Through life and death, hath now to glory gone,
  He sends His messengers to lead us on,
          The way is broad and plain!"

"Whither, oh, whither?"—"Terrible reply
  From yon white throne of judgment in the sky:
  'Depart, accursed! from My presence fly
          For ever'—awful word!"

"Whither, oh, whither?"—"Washed from earthly stain,
  No more to wander or to fall again;
  For ever with the Father to remain,
          For ever with the Lord!"

                              MÖWES.

SHADOW AND SUBSTANCE.

"Das Leben ist gleich einem Traum."

This life is like a flying dream,
Or like the vapour from the stream,
Or like the grass that grows to-day,
      But fades away
When winds across it roughly play.

Only Thyself, my God, art now
Just as Thou wert,—my Refuge Thou,—
Though rock and mountain be destroyed,
      There is no void,
With Thy loved presence still enjoyed.

Thus sojourning in this low scene,
Upon my Saviour I would lean,
And learn, as moments quickly fly,
      Self to deny,
Dead to the world, before I die.

Vain joys, away! yea, spread your wings!
For I have tasted better things.
I seek a portion all divine,
      For ever mine;
Lord Jesus, make me wholly Thine!

JOACHIM NEANDER.

THE MISSIONARY ON THE SEA-SHORE.

"Wie schäumt so feierlich zu unsern Füssen."

Dark mighty Ocean, rolling to our feet!
In thy low murmur many voices meet,
The sounds of distant lands, brought strangely near
          To Fancy's ear.

From shores unknown comes the sweet Sabbath bell,
New languages the old glad tidings tell,
We hear the hymn of praise,—the martyr's song,—
          All borne along.

And starting at the summons, we obey,
And o'er thy waves prepare to find our way;
Leaving the ties of country and of home,
          Ocean, we come!

Our chariot thou, to bear us to the lands
Where fields of promise wait our willing hands;
Thou and ourselves are servants, to fulfil
        Our Master's will!

And whether in thy depths we find a grave,
Or with our heart's-blood dye thy distant wave,
Or with glad hopes, upon thy billows borne,
        Homewards return;—

Whether to death or life our course leads on,—
The Master knows,—His holy will be done!
To life eternal, when all storms are past,
        We come at last!

F. DE LA MOTTE FOUQUE.

SABBATH MORNING HYMN.

"Hallelujah! Schöner Morgen!"

Hallelujah! Fairest morning,
  Fairer than my words can say!
Down I lay the heavy burden
  Of life's toil and care to-day;
While this morn of joy and love
Brings fresh vigour from above.

Sun-day, full of holy glory!
  Sweetest rest-day of the soul,
Light upon a world in darkness
  From thy blessed moments roll.
Holy, happy, heavenly day,
Thou canst charm my grief away!

Now, I taste my Father's goodness,
  Falling like the morning dew,
While of pastures even fairer
  I would take a distant view;

SABBATH MORNING HYMN.

Where my Shepherd's flock I see,
Where my dwelling soon shall be!

Oh, be silent, earthly turmoil!
   I have work more sweet and blest,
And each thought would gather homeward
   On this happy day of rest:
Thus with clearer faith to see
All my Lord has done for me.

In the gladness of His worship,
   I will seek my joy to-day:
It is then I learn the fulness
   Of the grace for which I pray;
When the word of life is given,
Like the Saviour's voice from heaven.

Let the day's sweet hours be ended
   Prayerfully, as they've begun;
And Thy blessing, Lord, be granted,
   Till earth's days and weeks are done,
That at last Thy servant may
Keep eternal Sabbath day.

SCHMOLK.

CHARITY.

"Christ! wenn die Armen manchesmal."

Ah, Christian, if the needy poor
    Have e'er unheeded been,
Beware, lest at thy closed door
    The Saviour stood unseen!

Let heart and house be open thrown,
    Thy gifts with others share;
Let holy charity be shown
    To all who need thy care.

Then, while thy glance abroad is cast,
    The Lord is by thy side;
For through the open door He passed,
    When it was opened wide.

And ere thy beating heart can guess
    Who entered by the door,
His gracious hands are raised to bless
    Thy basket and thy store;

To bless thee all time's little day,
   With His almighty love;
To bless the long eternity
   That waits for thee above,—

Where soon the pearly gates which stand,
   To all He'll open throw
Who, for His sake, with willing hand,
   Did minister below.

                      HEY.

WE TOO ARE THINE.

"Herr, unser Gott, mit Ehrfurcht dienen."

Lord our God, in reverence lowly,
The hosts of heaven call Thee "holy;"
From cherubim and seraphim,
From angel phalanx, far extending,
In fuller tones is still ascending
The "holy, holy," of their hymn.
  The fount of joy Thou art,
  Ever filling every heart,
    Ever! ever!
We too are Thine, and with them sing,
"Thou, Lord, and only Thou art King."

Lord, there are bending now before Thee
The elders, with their crownëd glory,
The first-born of the blessed band.
There, too, earth's ransomed and forgiven,
Brought by the Saviour safe to heaven,
In glad unnumbered myriads stand.

WE TOO ARE THINE.

  Loud are the songs of praise
  Their mingled voices raise,
    Ever! ever!
We too are Thine, and with them sing,
" Thou, Lord, and only Thou art King."

They sing, in sweet and sinless numbers,
The wondrous love that never slumbers;
And of the wisdom, power, and might,
The truth and faithfulness abiding,
And over all Thy works presiding.
But they can scarcely praise aright;
  For all is never sung,
  Even by seraph's tongue—
    Never! never!
We too are Thine, and with them sing,
" Thou, Lord, and only Thou art King."

Oh! come, reveal Thyself more fully,
That we may learn to praise more truly;
Make every heart a temple true,
Filled with Thy glory overflowing,
More of Thy love each morning showing,
And waking praises loud and new,—

Here let Thy peace divine
Over Thy children shine,
Ever! ever!
And glad or sad, we still shall sing,
"Thou, Lord, and only Thou art King."

G. TERSTEEGEN.

SUBMISSION.

"Du sollst," so sprach der Herr, "du sollst ermatten."

Thus said the Lord—"Thy days of health are over!"
And, like the mist, my vigour fled away;
Till but a feeble shadow was remaining,
A fragile form, fast hasting to decay.
The May of life, with all its blooming flowers,—
The joys of life, in colours bright arrayed,—
The hopes of life, in all their airy promise,—
I saw them in the distance slowly fade:
  Then sighs of sorrow in my soul would rise,
  Then silent tears would overflow my eyes!
But a warm sunbeam, from a higher sphere,
Stole through the gloom, and dried up every tear;—
Is this Thy will, good Lord?—the strife is o'er,
  Thy servant weeps no more.

"Thy cherished flock thou mayest feed no longer!"—
 Thus said the Lord, who gave them to my hand;

Nor even was my sinking heart permitted
To ask the reason of the stern command.
The Shepherd's rod had been so gladly carried,
The flock had followed long, and loved it well:
Alas! the hour was dark, the stroke was heavy,
When sudden from my nerveless grasp it fell.
  Then sighs of sorrow in my soul would rise,
  Then rushing tears would overflow my eyes!
But I beheld *Thee*, O my Lord and God,
Beneath the Cross, lay down the Shepherd's rod;—
Is this Thy will, good Lord?—the strife is o'er,
  Thy servant weeps no more.

"*Never again* thou mayest feed My people!"—
Thus said the Lord, with countenance severe;
And bade me lay aside, at once, for ever,
The robes of office, honoured long and dear.
The sacred mantle from my shoulders falling,—
The sacred girdle loosening at His word,—
I could but think and say, while sadly gazing,
I *have been* once a pastor of the Lord!
  Then groans of anguish in my soul would rise,
  Then burning tears would overflow my eyes!—
But His own garment once was torn away,
To the rude soldiery a spoil and prey;—

SUBMISSION.

Is this Thy will, good Lord?—the strife is o'er,
    Thy servant weeps no more.

"From the calm port of safety rudely severed,
    Through stormy waves thy shattered bark must go,
And dimly see, amid the darkness sinking,
    Nothing but heaven above and depths below!"—
Thus said the Lord,—and through a raging ocean
    Of doubts and fears my spirit toiled in vain.
Ah! many a dove went forth, of hope inquiring,
    But none with olive leaf returned again!
        Then groans of anguish in my soul would rise,
        Then tears of bitterness o'erflowed my eyes!—
But through the gloom the promised light was given,
    From the dark waves I *could* look up to heaven;—
Is this Thy will, good Lord?—the strife is o'er,
    Thy servant weeps no more.

"Thou shalt find kindred hearts, in love united,
    And with them in the wilderness rejoice.
Yet stand prepared, each gentle tie untwining,
    To separate, at My commanding voice!"—
Thus said the Lord.—He gave, as He had promised,—
    How many a loving heart has met my own!
But—ever must the tender bonds be broken,
    And each go forwards, distant and alone!

Then sighs of sorrow in my soul would rise,
Then tears of anguish overflowed my eyes!—
But Thou hast known the bitter parting day,
From the beloved John hast turned away;—
Is this Thy will, good Lord?—the strife is o'er,
Thy servant weeps no more.

Möwes.

These stanzas were written by the devoted pastor, Heinrich Möwes, in 1832, when obliged by illness to resign the ministerial office.

A PASTOR'S PARTING WORDS.

"Merkt ihr's, Freunde!"

Hear me, my friends! the hour has come,
Soon I must leave you, and hasten home;
Then, ere our Father shall call me to rest,
Hear my last wishes, my last request.

When my last moments on earth draw near,
When my own voice you no longer hear,
Then gather round me, and sing the song
We have sung together and loved so long.

Sing of His love who has died to save,
Him who has entered and spoiled the grave;
Sing with glad accents and grateful heart,
Sing, till my spirit in peace depart.

Fold my cold hands on my quiet breast,
Close my tired eyelids in gentle rest,
One farewell kiss of affection take,—
Leave me till Christ shall my slumber break.

To our last dwelling-place bear me along
With sweetest music of chimes and song;
There let the evergreen branches wave,
And bright flowers blossom around my grave.

Though a long darkness has veiled my eyes,
Still let them look to the eastern skies;
There, where the Morning Star rose bright,
Jesus, the Sun of our darkest night.

Carve but these words on the simple stone—
"*Living and dying, of Jesus alone*
Ever he spoke to the Church beneath;
Sweet to him, therefore, was life and death."

When ye revisit the peaceful spot,
Come with soft tears and with tender thought;
Look up to heaven in hope and prayer,
Jesus again will unite us there!

MÖWES.

BE THOU MY FRIEND.

"Sey du mein Freund."

Be Thou my Friend, and look upon my heart,
    Lord Jesus, Son of man!
Each seed of good or ill that there has part
    Do Thou in mercy scan.
  The burning springs there lurking,
    O Lord, Thou canst control,
  And each wild passion, working
    Within my sinful soul.

In mortal weakness, once was veiled Thy might,
    Light of Eternal Day!
Before Thee lay temptation's dreary fight,
    And yet,—Thou wentst that way!
  And Thou couldst weep with sorrow,
    Or share our bridal mirth,
  And yet no tarnish borrow
    From this polluted earth.

Beneath Thy feet the realms of earth were spread,
    All bathed in golden gloss;
One word had laid their crowns upon Thy head,
    Yet,—Thou couldst choose the cross!
  And from Thy throne descending,
    Couldst take the pilgrim's path,
  And with Thy hosts attending,
    Couldst die a shameful death!

How the world hated Thee, and vengeance hurled
    Against Thee,—great Unknown!
How Thou didst love this poor and blinded world,
    And bought her for Thine own!
  Her arrows piercëd through Thee,
    From cruel, willing hands;
  Yet Thou wouldst draw her to Thee
    With loving, gentle bands.

Thou hast returned, all pure and holy, home,
    My Brother, and my Lord!
And when with trembling to Thy throne I come,
    My Refuge is Thy word.
  There, by Thine arm fast holding,
    And hidden, by Thy grace,
  Within Thy robe's deep folding,
    Let me behold God's face.

BE THOU MY FRIEND.

Yes! be my Friend, and look upon my heart,
   On all that's hidden there;
The deeper guilt that stings me with its dart,
   The unknown sins I bear,
    The passions that distress me,
     Let Thy pure presence slay;
    The sorrows that oppress me
     Before Thee flee away.

Oh, shine upon me with Thy holy light,
   When gathering gloom I see,
And leave me not in tribulation's night,
   But send sweet peace to me!
    The chains of sin dissever,
     Bind fancy's wildest play;
    At last, my Lord, for ever
     Take grief and sin away!

                    LANGE.

AS THOU WILT.

"Wie Gott will! also will ich sagen."

As Thou wilt, my God! I ever say;
   What Thou wilt is ever best for me;
What have I to do with earthly care,
   Since to-morrow I may leave with Thee?
Lord, Thou knowest, I am not my own,
All my hope and help depend on Thee alone.

As Thou wilt! still I can believe;
   Never did the word of promise fail.
Faith can hold it fast, and feel it sure,
   Though temptations cloud and fears assail.
Why art thou disquieted, O my soul?
When thy Father knows, and rules the whole.

As Thou wilt! still I can endure;
   Patiently my daily cross can bear;
Why should I complain, a pardoned child,
   If the children's portion here I share?
As Thou wilt, my Father and my God!
I can drink the cup, and kiss the rod.

AS THOU WILT.

As Thou wilt! still I can hope on:
   Sunshine may return when storms have past;
Thine All-seeing Eye of sleepless love
   Watches o'er my path from first to last.
When Thou wilt, upon the desert plain
Springs may rise anew and rivers flow again.

As Thou wilt! all life's journey through,
   To Thy will my own I would resign:
If on earth I have but little store,
   Be it so! all heaven shall be mine;
Or if but Thyself, my God, art given,
Nothing more I need or ask in earth or heaven.

As Thou wilt! when Thine hour has come,
   Let Thy servant, Lord, in peace depart;
Good it is to love and serve Thee here,
   Better to be with Thee where Thou art.
When, or where, or how the call may be,
It will not come too early or too late for me.

As Thou wilt, O Lord! I ask no more.
   With the promise, Faith pursues her way;
Patience can endure through sorrow's night,
   Hope can look beyond, to heaven's own day,
Love can wait, and trust, and labour still;—
Life and death shall be according to Thy will!

NEUMEISTER.

SABBATH HYMN.

"Zeige Dich uns ohne Hülle."

Lord, remove the veil away,
Let us see Thyself to-day!
Thou who camest from on high,
For our sins to bleed and die,
Help us now to cast aside
All that would our hearts divide;
With the Father and the Son
Let Thy living Church be one.

Oh, from earthly cares set free,
Let us find our rest in Thee!
May our toils and conflicts cease
In the calm of Sabbath peace,
That Thy people here below
Something of the bliss may know,
Something of the rest and love
In the Sabbath-home above.

SABBATH HYMN.

From beyond the grave's dark night
What mild radiance meets my sight?
Softly stealing on the ear,
What strange music do I hear?
'Tis the golden crowns on high,
'Tis the chorus of the sky!
Lord, Thy sinful child prepare
For a place and portion there!

Give my soul the spotless dress
Of Thy perfect righteousness;
Then at length, a welcome guest,
I shall enter to the feast,
Take the harp, and raise the song,
All Thy ransomed ones among;
Earthly cares and sorrows o'er,
Joys to last for evermore!

KLOPSTOCK.

WHAT PLEASES GOD.

" Was Gott gefällt, mein frommes Kind."

What God decrees, child of His love,
Take patiently, though it may prove
The storm that wrecks thy treasure here ;—
Be comforted! thou needst not fear
    What pleases God.

The wisest will is God's own will:
Rest on this anchor, and be still;
For peace around thy path shall flow,
When only wishing here below
    What pleases God.

Oh! could I sing, as I desire,
My grateful voice should never tire
To tell the wondrous love and power,
Thus working out, from hour to hour.
    What pleases God.

WHAT PLEASES GOD.

The King of kings, He rules on earth,
He sends us sorrow here, or mirth;
All nature bows to His command,
And thus we meet, on sea or land,
    What pleases God.

His Church on earth He dearly loves,
Although He oft her sin reproves:
The rod itself His love can speak;
He smites till we return to seek
    What pleases God.

Then let the crowd around thee seize
The joys that for a season please,
But willingly their paths forsake,
And for thy blessed portion take
    What pleases God.

Thy heritage is safe in heaven:
There shall the crown of joy be given;
There shalt thou hear, and see, and know,
As thou couldst never here below,
    What pleases God.

GERHARDT.

AT LAST.

"Zuletzt geht's wohl."

At last all shall be well with those, His own,
   Whom Christ from sin and Satan has made free;
   At last shall come the year of jubilee,
The time of rest, when all their fears are flown.

At last shall come the glory and reward,
   When we have stood the world's reproach and loss,
   When faith and love have meekly borne the cross,
And the good servants are made like their Lord.

At last the soldier shall receive his crown,
   Brought from the field, home to his fatherland;
   For ever in a peaceful lot to stand,
His foes all vanquished, and his arms laid down.

At last the water shall be turned to wine,
   And all the marriage guests, in bliss above,
   The wonders trace of God's redeeming love,
His counsels all fulfilled, and plans divine.

AT LAST.

At last, not yet, into the heavenly rest
   The Lord shall lead His saints, and give them there,
   Made like the angels, angel joys to share,
Ever with Him and with each other blest.

At last, not yet;—O weary heart, be still!
   Trust to thy God, thy Saviour, and thy Friend,
   Who chastens now, but loves unto the end.
So be it, Lord! good is Thy holy will.

C. A. BERNSTEIN.

THE GRAVEYARD.

"Ich weiss ein stilles, liebes Land."

I know a sweet and silent spot,
   Where gladly oft I stay,
Though many near me heed it not,
   Or wish it far away.

'Tis but a narrow strip of land,
   Hedged in, and decked with flowers;
Yet all around it tokens stand
   Of other world than ours.

These little mounds men scarcely see,
   Nor dream of gold concealed;
But they are precious mines to me,
   Where treasures vast are sealed.

Here, as beside some boundary-stone,
   The child of troubled time
Looks upward, where his friends are gone,
   And seeks their brighter clime.

THE GRAVEYARD.

Here, I have gathered strength and light
   For all my future way;
Here, faith is nearly turned to sight,
   And night almost to day.

And not afar, I see the day
   Which daily draws more near,
When passing friends shall pause, and say,
"Our brother's grave is here!"

But I'll have journeyed, glad and free,
   Far from this silent spot,
While leaving to its sanctuary
   What others' hands have brought;

And in my Father's happy land
   Have met my own once more,
Where we shall scarcely understand
   Why we have wept before.

LANGE.

FUNERAL HYMN.

"Lebwohl! die Erde wartet dein."

BELOVED and honoured, fare thee well!
Go in thy last long home to dwell;
Softly our loving hands prepare
Thy narrow bed,—sleep softly there!

Love looks below, with weeping eyes,
Where her long-cherished treasure lies.
Our sweet companionship is o'er,
Our pilgrim friend returns no more!

Earth takes her own—this mortal frame;
Eternity her part shall claim;
And so we say, in humble trust,
The soul to God—the dust to dust.

Then, looking up through sorrow's night,
We trace the spirit's homeward flight;
The Prince of Life has marked that road,
Through the dark valley, home to God.

FUNERAL HYMN.

Where once the Master lowly lay,
Let the tired servant rest to-day,
And in the Father's house above
For ever share his Master's love.

Thanks for thy joy, all danger past!
Thanks for our own good hope at last!
Weeping endureth for a night,
Joy cometh with the morning light.

Lord, will that morning soon appear?
May our own summons now be near?
Shall sorrow soon be past and gone?
Thy will be done! Thy will be done!

Only prepare us, all Thy will
Gladly to suffer, or fulfil;
Then call us to Thy heavenly rest,
With Thee, and with our brother blest.

F. SACHSE.

MINISTERING ANGELS.

"Um die Erd' und um ihr Kinder."

Round this earth and round her children
    Floats a spirit land unseen.
When our earthly course is ended,
    When the veil shall rise between,
When we cross this mortal threshold,
    When we take our heavenward way,
Angel brothers shall uphold us—
    Brothers of Eternity.

God's own children, pure and holy!
    You the messengers He sends;
'Tis an ever sweet remembrance,
    That you are our guardian friends,—
That you watch our life-long journey,
    That, unseen, you oft are near,
Holy thoughts and deeds to strengthen,
    Or to dry the mourner's tear.

Who would not retreat in terror
    From the evil yet undone;
Who not turn with shame and mourning
    From the evil course begun;
Who would e'er be found forgetful
    Of his calling and his vow,
If the thought had only risen,
" Angels are among us now "?

Rise, my soul, in heart to meet them,
    When this earth would chain thee fast;
Rise among these free-born spirits,
    When her coils are round thee cast.
Be courageous, 'tis thy journey
    Out of darkness into light;
God and angels are around thee,
    Tremble not, but rise and fight.

SPERL.

THE MIDNIGHT CRY.

"Der Herr bricht an, um Mitternacht."

The Lord shall come in dead of night,
    When all is stillness round;
How happy they whose lamps are bright,
    Who hail the trumpet's sound!

How blind and dead the world appears!
    How deep her slumbers are!
Still dreaming that the day she fears
    Is distant and afar.

Who spends his day in holy toil,
    His talent used aright,
That he may haste, with heavenly spoil,
    To meet his Lord that night?

Who is arousing from their sleep
    The saints who dare to rest,
And calling every one to keep
    A watch more true and blest?

THE MIDNIGHT CRY.

Wake up, my heart and soul, anew,
    Let sleep no moment claim;
But hourly watch, as if ye knew
    This night the Master came.

The Lord shall come in dead of night,
    When all is stillness round;
How happy they whose lamps are bright,
    Who hail the trumpet's sound!

ZINZENDORF.

YET THERE IS ROOM.

"Es ist noch Raum!"

Yet there is room! room in His house to fill,
   Though countless hosts appear;
See, at His table vacant places still,
   Oh, waited-guests, draw near!
Forsake your vain and fading pleasures,
And take His offered, boundless treasures:
               Yet there is room!

Yet there is room! The many ransomed there
   Suffice not for His love;
He longs that every one His grace would share,
   His saving mercy prove;
For still He stands with sinners pleading,
His voice in heaven still interceding.
               Yet there is room!

Yet there is room! O sinner, pause again,
   Think of this call once more;

Or is your heart so closed, that Christ in vain
   Stands knocking at the door?
All His long-offered love discarded,
Himself a stranger disregarded,
               Who finds no room?

Yet there is room! Oh shame, to feel no need,
   No hungering after good,
Content upon these empty husks to feed,
   So near to heavenly food!
Food, offered still if you accept it;
But know, for those who will reject it,
               There is no room!

Yet there is room! O sinner, hear it still,
   And then the words repeat!—
Come, feeble, weak, despairing if you will,
   Come to the Saviour's feet.
Say, "Jesus, give! in full surrender,
I come my worthless heart to tender—
               An empty room."

Yet there is room! When earth can give no more
   A dwelling to her guest,
Thank God! the Christian sees a brighter shore
   And home of endless rest.

It is enough, when death is nearing,
This blest assurance to be hearing,
Yet there is room!

Yet there is room! a heavenly dwelling-place,
   How infinitely wide!
There rests the soul, beholding Jesus' face,
   And fully satisfied.
The flock, who follow Him through sadness,
Are gathering there in holy gladness.
Yet there is room!
C. G. Woltersdorf.

COMFORT.

"O wie manche, schöne Stunde."

O how many hours of beauty
    Has the Master dealt around!
O how many broken spirits
    Has He tenderly upbound!

O how often, to refresh us,
    Warmly beams the sun of life,
Chasing from our brows the furrows
    Gathered in its gloom and strife.

Thus it will go on for ever,
    Till the end of all things here;
Till our Lord to glory call us,
    In His presence to appear.

Then the Fatherland to enter,
    And no more as pilgrims drest,
But adorned with all the shining
    Festal raiment of the blest.

COMFORT.

Should not this thy spirit strengthen
    To rejoice, be calm and still,
And to follow where He leadeth,
    Let Him lead thee where He will?

All things work for thy salvation,
    If indeed thou art His friend:
Tarry but a little season,
    Only wait until the end.

Doubtless rugged heights arising
    Fill thy heart with deep alarms;
But where thou canst not surmount them,
    Christ will bear thee in His arms.

Only journey ever onward,
    Further on the homeward way,
Ever with an eye uplifted
    To the clearer realms of day.

Fearless thou mayest tread the valley,
    All in shadow though it be,
When the open blue of heaven
    Shines beyond the gloom for thee.

                                SPITTA.

THE MISSIONARY'S FAREWELL.

"Ich stehe noch auf heimathliche Strande."

Still on the shores of home my feet are standing,
   But home itself even now behind me lies;
Still my ship's anchor holds—but fast are breaking
   Round this sad heart the dearest, strongest ties.

Slowly and painfully those bonds are parting,
   Now only known to clasp so close, so strong;—
Fain would the tree grow on, nor bear transplanting
   From the loved soil where it has stood so long!

Yonder, where I must go, the earth and heaven
   Another aspect will appear to wear,
A fiercer sun will shine in noonday splendour,
   And stars unknown light up the darkness there.

The cradle-song, which soothed my childhood's slumbers,
   The words of love and prayer, will sound no more;
All harsh will seem the unfamiliar accents
   Which greet the stranger on that distant shore.

THE MISSIONARY'S FAREWELL.

"Remain, remain!" I hear my dear ones calling,
    "Remain among us, loved and loving, still!
Tempt not the wild waves of the stormy ocean,
    Tempt not the blinded heathen's wilder will!"

Yes, I would stay, did I not hear another,
    A heavenly call, which tells me to depart:
His voice, who lingered not, when love and pity
    For helpless, hopeless sinners filled His heart—

His voice I hear; and theirs, the lost, the dying,—
    The wail of heathen anguish o'er the sea!
They must not perish thus, unheard, unheeded;
    The slaves of Satan must be yet set free!

Lord, I obey; I go, where Thou appointest,
    A willing servant, to the harvest field.
Nor will I turn again, my post forsaking,
    Though only thorns and briers the toil should yield.

The signal waves—Adieu, my own, my dearest!
    Remember in your prayers the absent one;
And mourn me not—ye know the Friend Almighty,
    All-wise, All-loving, who has with me gone!

                                                     MÖWES.

THE SHEPHERDS.

"Wo Lämmer schlafen."

WHERE the lambs sleep, there shepherds watch around;
  Where shepherds pray, there angels fill the plain;
  Where angels sing, heaven comes to earth again;
Where Jesus is, there heaven below is found.

The shepherds watch beneath the solemn sky,
  Looking above, till terror dims their view:
  "These blessed songs, come they, O stars, from you;
Or can a sinner's harp be tuned so high?"

On earth appeared a shining angel host,
  And thus their heavenly message, wondering, told:
    "To you the Saviour, Christ, is born to-day!"
    Forsaking all, the watchers speed away
  To seek their Shepherd, and to join His fold,—
Sure this glad night no little lamb is lost!

LANGE.

MORNING HYMN.

"Freund, komm in die Frühe."

Come at the morning hour,
Come, in Thy love and power,
   Friend of my heart!
For all the weary way,
And burdens of the day,
   Grace to impart.
     Thou makest bright
     The early light;
Give me strength in weakness, joy in toil,
   With Thy morning smile.

When from the noon-day heat
Fain would I make retreat,
   Come, gracious Lord;
Thy cheering blessing shed,
Thy soul-refreshments spread
   Around my board.

MORNING HYMN.

O heavenly Guest,
What peace, what rest,
With Thy presence comes, while all our care
Thou Thyself wilt bear!

When evening shadows fall,
And twilight steals o'er all,
Still be Thou near.
Sun, now withdraw thy light!
A radiance yet more bright
This heart can cheer.
The peace within,
Of pardoned sin,
Soul and spirit hushed in tranquil bliss,—
Where is rest like this?

When midnight darkness lies
Deep over earth and skies,
While thoughts of fear,
And evil spirits' power,
Make the mysterious hour
More dark and drear,—
My soul, be still,
Dread nought of ill;
Close, my eyes, in peace,—my heavenly Guard
Still keeps watch and ward.

MORNING HYMN.

  Let day proclaim to day,
  Night to night ever say,
   How he is blest
  Who can the Lord of all
  His God and Father call,
   And sweetly rest
   In quiet faith,
  Through life, through death,
Singing the songs on earth of praise and love,
  While angels join above!

UNBEKANNTES.

EVENING HYMN.

"*Der Tag ist hin.*"

The day departs:
My soul and heart
Long for that better morrow,
When Christ shall set His people free
From every care and sorrow.

The sunshine bright
Is lost in night:
O Lord, Thyself unveiling,
Shine on my soul, with beams of love,
All darkness there dispelling!

The noise of life,
Labour and strife,
Have come to calm cessation:
Let me Thy work of grace review,
In holy contemplation.

EVENING HYMN.

Now on my bed
I lay my head,
My weary eyelids closing:
Thus sweetly, Lord, my soul would rest,
On Thy sure love reposing.

Be Thou still nigh,
With sleepless eye,
While Thy poor child is sleeping;
And angel guards, at Thy command,
Afar all danger keeping.

This sun and moon,
This night and noon,
When shall their course be ending?
When shall the day eternal dawn
Whose sun has no descending?

The land above
Of peace and love,
No earthly beams need brighten;
For all its borders Christ Himself
Doth with His glory lighten.

Oh to be there,
That bliss to share,
Those hallelujahs singing!

With all the ransomed evermore
  My joyful praises bringing!

    Lord Jesus, Thou
    My refuge now,
Forsake Thy servant never!
Uphold and guide, till I may stand
  Before Thy face for ever!
J. A. FREYLINHAUSEN.

THE LITTLE FLOCK.

"Es kennt der Herr die Seinen."

He knoweth all His people,—
  From everlasting knew,—
The greatest and the smallest,
  The many and the few.
Not one of them shall perish,
  He guardeth each alone;
In living and in dying
  They shall remain His own.

The little flock He knoweth,—
  Who, though by faith not sight,
The Invisible are seeing,
  And trusting in His might.
Born by His word of power,
  And nourished by that word:
Within His storehouse finding
  The armour of their Lord.

And thus He knows His people,—
  By hope so bright and blest;
By faith that can its burden
  Upon the Saviour rest;
And by the look of gladness
  Where truth shines forth serene,
That plant which ever weareth
  An amaranthine green.

He knows them by their loving,—
  The fruit of His own love,
And by their earnest longing
  To please their Lord above;
By their long-suffering patience
  When others seek their ill;
By blessing as He blesseth,
  And bearing all His will.

And thus He knows His people,—
  From everlasting knew,—
The greatest and the smallest,
  The many and the few;
Where His own Spirit's working
  In gracious power is seen;
By faith, hope, love abounding,
  Where'er His step has been.

So help us, Lord, we pray Thee,
   Our goings thus uphold,
That none of glory rob us,
   Nor make our love grow cold;
That when the day of wonder
   Reveals Thy judgment throne,
We may look up rejoicing,
   Since numbered with Thine own.

SPITTA.

OUR ELIZA.

" Ich hatte der Kinder viere."

I HAD once four lovely children,
   And now I have three alone;
The fourth to the golden city
   Through the gate of death has gone.

My boy is still bright and blooming,
   And two of my daughters fair;
The third in her grave is lying—
   Ah, yes,—and I laid her there!

She lay, all her rosy blushes
   Now changed to the lilies pale;
She saw not her father weeping,
   She heard not her mother's wail.

Then her mother's arms resigned her
   To the last low place of rest,
And her father lifted to heaven
   The cry of a soul opprest.

OUR ELIZA.

Ah me! is she ours no longer,—
    Those lips with their smiles so sweet, —
The heaven in those blue eyes shining,
    The music of those small feet?

Didst thou know, O mighty Angel,
    When in the dread midnight hour
Thou camest, for Christ's own garden
    To gather our loveliest flower—

Didst thou know how our hearts were breaking?
    Did thine with compassion move?
Yes! yes! the land whence thou camest
    Is the land and home of love!

So with hearts resigned, though bleeding,
    We could yield her to thy care:
She has gone to the home of Jesus,
    We shall seek and find her there!

                              MÖWES.

EASTER HYMN.

"Hallelujah! Christus lebt!"

HALLELUJAH! Jesus lives!
   He is now the Living One.
From the gloomy house of death
   Forth the Conqueror has gone,
Bright Forerunner to the skies
Of His people, yet to rise.

Jesus lives! let all rejoice!
   Praise Him, ransomed ones of earth!
Praise Him, in a nobler song,
   Cherubim of heavenly birth;
Praise the Victor King, whose sway
Sin, and death, and hell obey.

Jesus lives! why weepest thou?
   Why that sad and frequent sigh?
He who died our Brother here,
   Lives our Brother still on high,—

Lives for ever, to bestow
Blessings on His Church below.

Jesus lives! and thus, my soul,
    Life eternal waits for thee:
Joined to Him, thy living Head,
    Where He is thou too shalt be;
With Himself, at His right hand,
Victor over death shalt stand.

Jesus lives! to Him my heart
    Draws with ever new delight:
Earthly vanities, depart!
    Hinder not my heavenward flight!
Let this spirit ever rise
To its magnet in the skies.

Hallelujah! angels, sing,
    Join us in our hymn of praise!
Let your chorus swell the strain
    Which our feebler voices raise:
Glory to our God above,
And on earth His peace and love!

C. B. GARVE.

"WE ARE THE LORD'S."

"Wir sind des Herrn's."

We are the Lord's!—in life, in death remaining,
   We are the Lord's, the Crucified, the Son.
We are the Lord's, the mighty King now reigning,
   We are the Lord's, who fought for us and won.

We are the Lord's!—His holy name thus naming,
   Ours be the life that with His name accords,
By thought, by speech, by deed, each day proclaiming,
   Louder than words can speak, "We are the Lord's."

We are the Lord's!—and when our souls are treading
   The dreary valley, then these precious words
Disperse its gloom, a holy radiance shedding,
   And we will fear no ill,—"We are the Lord's."

We are the Lord's !—if the last foe alarm us,
  That mighty arm draws near and help affords;
And death has lost his sting, his power to harm us,
  When we can calmly say, "We are the Lord's."
SPITTA.

LOVE AND THE CROSS.

"Liebe und ein Kreuz dazu."

Love and a cross, together blest,
Bring to the Christian peace and rest:
Too sweet were love, if felt alone;
Too sad the cross, with love unknown.

And so the two together come,
Sent by our God to lead us home,
And guide within the narrow way
Our footsteps, ever prone to stray.

For love, when it is sent alone,
And pain and sorrow all unknown,
With soft enchantments fills the heart,
And steals from heaven its rightful part.

Without a cross, love is but blind,
And fond illusions cloud the mind;
Until by sorrow's light we view
Realities, of false and true.

But when a cross is felt alone,
And all the joys of love unknown,
The heart, oppressed without relief,
May sink beneath its load of grief;

For cares and burdens doubly press,—
Sorrow has added bitterness,—
All hope and courage seem to fly,
While dark despair is drawing nigh.

But love with gentle smile comes near,
Despair and darkness disappear;
While strength and energy she brings
To do or suffer wondrous things.

Then give me, Lord,—I ask no more,—
These blessings, from Thy wondrous store,
Love and the cross: of these possest,
I am and shall be ever blest.

UNBEKANNTES.

MY BELOVED IS MINE, AND I AM HIS.

"Liebe, die um mich zum Bilde."

Loved One! who by grace hast wrought me
   Somewhat to Thy likeness pure—
Loved One! who in mercy sought me,
   Lost and wretched, blind and poor—
Loved One! hear me vow, this day,
To be Thine eternally.

Loved One! who in heaven chose me
   Ere creation found me here—
Loved One! who once stooped so lowly,
   As among us to appear—
Loved One! hear me vow, this day,
To be Thine eternally.

Loved One! who endured such anguish,
   Who for man so toiled and bled—
Loved One! who by death didst vanquish
   All my foes, and in my stead—

Loved One! hear me vow, this day,
To be Thine eternally.

Loved One! who art now bestowing
  Light and knowledge, truth and grace—
Loved One! who Thyself art showing
  As the sinner's hiding-place—
Loved One! hear me vow, this day,
To be Thine eternally.

Loved One! who for ever loves me,
  Still for me in heaven prays—
Loved One! who my freedom gives me,
  And the mighty ransom pays—
Loved One! hear me vow, this day,
To be Thine eternally.

Loved One! who, ere long, wilt wake me
  From the grave, where I shall lie—
Loved One! who, ere long, wilt make me
  Sharer of Thy bliss on high—
Loved One! hear me vow, this day,
To be Thine eternally.

JOHANN SCHEFFLER.

"ONE THING IS NEEDFUL."

"Ach! das Herz verlassend Alles."

Ah! the heart that has forsaken
   All things to secure the one,
In the secret of its chambers
   Finds the joy of heaven begun.

Ah! the heart that is contented
   Nought to know save God alone,
In the fulness of His blessing
   Finds a peace before unknown.

Ah! the heart that once has bathëd
   In Salvation's boundless sea,
In its waters drops the burden
   Of a lifetime's misery.

Ah! the heart that lives dissevered
   From the vain delights of time,
By a peaceful path is treading
   Through this vale of tears and crime.

"ONE THING IS NEEDFUL."

O that thus we could surrender
    Worldly pomp, and pride, and show,
Seeking Him in whom is centred
    All of good that man can know!

O that thus His blessed presence
    In our hearts we here enjoyed!
For without Him all is dreary,—
    Earth is dark, and vain, and void.

O that thus our eyes were resting
    Evermore on Christ our King,
Until conscience lose its burden,
    Life its load, and death its sting!

O Thou Fount of every blessing,
    Draw us, by the cross, till we,
Heart and soul, and will and spirit,
    Are for ever one with Thee!

                        UNBEKANNTES.

CONFESSION.

"Du treues Gott! ich sag es mit Empfindung."

O FAITHFUL GOD! with deep and sad emotion,
   My selfish waywardness I now confess,
Mourning o'er vows and resolutions broken,
   And oft resistings of Thy Spirit's grace.
How sad and comfortless the retrospection
   Of wasted days and years, for ever gone,
Plans unaccomplished all, and paths forsaken,
   Where Faith and Hope once beckoned brightly on!

Here is my heart! oh, keep the gift for ever!
   So often given, and recalled again,—
So often raised before in high aspirings,
   Then downward drawn by follies wild and vain!
How just were now Thy holy indignation,
   Telling that mercy's day of grace was o'er;
But Thou "upbraidest not," oh, still be gracious,
   Speak the kind words of hope, "Begin once more!"

                            MORAVIAN.

GRATITUDE.

"Wie gross ist der Allmächt'gen Gute."

How great Jehovah's love, how tender!
   He hath no heart who sits unmoved,
Stifling the thanks that he should render,
   Nor ever thinks that he is loved.
Yes! and that love to fathom, ever
   Shall be my first, my earnest thought.
This mighty Lord forgets me never:
   Oh, then, my soul, forget Him not!

Who has my wondrous lot provided?
   The Lord, who had no need of me.
Who has my stumbling footsteps guided?
   He whom I tried to shun and flee.
Who with new strength revived my spirit?
   And who this inward peace has given?
Who gives me all things to inherit?
   Who, but the Lord of earth and heaven!

GRATITUDE.

Above this life in spirit bounding,
    Behold, my soul, the heavenly bliss,
Where thou, God's glory all surrounding,
    Shall ever see Him as He is!
These joys thou shalt be soon possessing,
    Thy right shall never be denied;
For, lo! to win for thee the blessing,
    The Saviour came, and lived, and died

Then shall I not, in glad allegiance,
    To God the Lord my homage pay;
And when He calls, with swift obedience,
    Go where I see Him point the way?
His love, within my heart now reigning,
    Leads me to duties hid before;
And though I fail, through sin remaining,
    It shall not have dominion more.

Here, then, my Saviour, let me ever
    More of Thy love and goodness see,
To strengthen every weak endeavour
    That dedicates my life to Thee;
To cheer when sorrow clouds my dwelling,
    To keep me safe in joy's bright day,
And all my fears of guilt dispelling,
    To take the sting of death away.

PAUL GELLERT.

PRAYER.

"Die Einfalt spricht von Herzen."

The simple-hearted pray,
In joy and grief, alway,—
Not careful how to choose
What sounding words to use.

Thus little children pray,
And who receive as they?
Their childlike, lisping speech,
A father's heart must reach.

So let us, in our need,
With our Great Father plead,
And with no servile fear,
No slavish dread, draw near.

The sigh without a word,
The brief, "Have mercy, Lord!"
Knocks straightway at His door,
Brings blessing evermore.

Though, when the heart o'erflows,
And scarce a limit knows,
And pleading still we stay,
He will not turn away;

Yet when I little say,
When grief must have its way,
When scarce one word will come
Because my heart seems dumb,

But still my hands I reach
As one bereft of speech,
And dare to raise my eye
For mercy from on high,—

My prayers and my sighs
Alike before Him rise,
And by His love are found,
That knows no mortal bound.

F. G. WOLTERSDORF.

THE FATHER KNOWS THEE.

"Der Vater kennt dich!"

The Father knows thee! Learn of Him,
    And strive to see Him clearer;
When clouds are round thee, dark and dim,
    Draw nearer then, draw nearer.
        If thou art His,
        How good it is!
Let not the world ashame thee,
He for His child will claim thee.

The Father knows thee! Is thy care
    Hid in the heart's recesses?
A Father's eye has seen it there,
    Tell Him thy deep distresses.
        Pour out thy soul,
        Unveil the whole,
Believer; of thy weeping
The Father count is keeping.

THE FATHER KNOWS THEE.

The Father knows thee! and thy lot
  He hath prepared and blesseth;
And canst thou dream the child forgot
  Who once such love possesseth?
      Never afar
      His mercies are:
When trials thickly gather,
Help cometh from the Father.

The Father knows thee! All unseen,
  Wert thou the weary tending?
Or have thy thoughts to heaven been
  In solitude ascending?
      Each silent deed
      His eye can read;
No thought, that rose unbidden,
From Him was ever hidden.

The Father knows thee! Let no sin
  In guilt again enchain thee,
But may the Presence thou art in
  For evermore restrain thee.
      No futile lies,
      No false disguise
Avail, where He is dwelling,
'Mid light all clouds dispelling.

                  UNBEKANNTES.

JESUS THE WAY.

"Aus irdischem Getümmel."

Amid this world's commotion,
   When hearts all failing seem,
Who points the way to heaven,
   Where hope again shall beam?
Who brings us through the conflict?
   Who guides us when we stray?
Who leads through death to glory?
   Jesus,—Himself the Way.

Here wandering on and stumbling,
   And veiled in deepest night,
Where shall our souls discover
   A true and lasting light?
From heaven the sunshine cometh
   That all things brighten can,—
Jesus Himself revealeth
   The only Light for man.

Who gives us joy already,
  Which none can take away?
Who shows us, in our sorrow,
  The coming dawn of day?
When death is seen approaching,
  Who quells the spirit's strife?
Who leads us to the Father?
  Jesus,—Himself the Life.

ARNDT.

COMMUNION.

"Kommt herein, ihr lieben Glieder."

FRIENDS in Jesus, now draw near,
Brothers, sisters, enter here;
Filled with humble, glad emotion,
Bowed in lowly, deep devotion.

Come, approach the sacred board,
'Tis the Supper of the Lord,
Where the choicest things of heaven
From His loving heart are given.

He who, leaving throne and crown,
To our fallen world came down,
All our wants and woes to share,
All our sins and griefs to bear,—

He who journeyed weary years
In the land of toil and tears,

Onward to the cross and grave
Hastening, the lost to save,—

He devised this feast of love,
Thus the coldest heart to move,
Thus to bring Himself more near,
Thus to make Himself more dear.

On the sacred symbols feasting,
All the love of Jesus tasting,
All the Spirit's grace and power,—
O the sweetness of the hour!

Who can tell the joy, the bliss,
Of communion such as this!
Sink, my soul, in deep prostration,
Lowly, fervent adoration!

Earth-bound hearts, at length arise!
Reason, soar beyond the skies!
At Thine altar, Lord, we bend,
Let the fire from heaven descend!

Hush your anthems, cherubim!
Stand astonished, seraphim!
Men on earth, your brothers lowly,
Dare to join your "Holy! Holy!"

Lord, may grace imparted here
In our future lives appear;
"These have been," let others say,
"At the gates of heaven to-day."

COUNT ZINZENDORF.

THOU KNOWEST THAT I LOVE THEE.

"Ein seliges Herz führ't diese Sprache."

When towards heaven my best affections move,
Sweet is the thought—my business is *to love*,
To love with all my soul, and heart, and might.
Him who for me endured life's toil and sorrow,
    And death's dark night.

He ever loves,—how full the proof He gave,
Coming the lost of earth to seek and save!
He loves the captives whom He died to free,
He loves the Church, He loves the little children,
    Loves even me.

He felt, as we can feel, when heart with heart
In deepest, truest sympathies has part;
Loving with all, but with a favoured few—
O Mary! John! how blessed was your portion,
    How He loved you!

And wilt Thou love me also, gracious Friend—
Love me, as him who on Thy bosom leaned?
Then with the weeping Magdalene the while
I will embrace Thy feet, in hope awaiting
  One word, one smile!

Weeping, when Thou art absent, like a child
Left by its mother lonely in the wild;
Oh, when Thy Spirit's voice no more I hear,
Nor feel Thy presence, all around is sadness,
  All dark and drear!

Long this poor sinful heart Thou must have known,
By many a loving sigh, and mourning groan.
Thy gifts of faith and hope may brightly shine,
But love is more,—it seems to bring possession,
  It makes Thee mine.

And how am I thus blest? Thy grace alone,
Thy wondrous mercy, chose me for Thine own.
I sought Thee not, when Thou wert seeking me;
Thy love went forth, the helpless wanderer finding.
  Who loves like Thee?

MORAVIAN.

THE MORNING OF JOY.

"Morgen soll es besser werden."

Yes! it shall be well at morning,—
    'Tis the promise, strong and true.
Meekly bear thy earthly burden,
    With our Lord and heaven in view.

Yes! it can be well at morning,—
    Heavenly wisdom knoweth how;
Though to human sight are failing
    Every hope and comfort now.

Yes! it must be well at morning;
    For His flock, within the fold,
All the truth and might of Jesus
    Have been guaranteed to hold.

Yes! it shall be well at morning,—
    Faith has made this truth thine own,—

And thy pilgrimage of sorrow
  Must be leading to the throne.

Morning! loved and looked-for morning!
  Morning of eternal light!
Thou wilt chase these clouds of trouble,
  Thou wilt end the gloom of night!
C. B. GARVE.

THE TWO CALLS.

"Hier bin ich, Herr! du rufest mir."

Here am I, Lord, Thou callest me,
Thou drawest and I follow Thee;
My heart and soul Thou dost demand —
I lay them gladly in Thy hand.

It is my grief to come so late,
Thy mercy had so long to wait;
It is my joy that love divine
Could look upon a heart like mine.

I dare not linger,—duties rise,
Before unseen, to meet my eyes;
Contrite, I haste my Lord to meet—
But, ah, how laggard move these feet!

I am as Peter was of old:
Before the storm I stood so bold,—

It comes—I sink; ah! stretch Thy hand
And draw the trembler safe to land.

Once Thou didst call; but now, Lord, hear
The prayer that fain would reach Thine ear;—
"Oh, lead me to the Rock," I cry,
"The Rock that higher is than I!"

Shed down on me Thy mighty power,
To strengthen for each coming hour;
And then through flood, through fire and sword,
I'll follow Thee, my Lord, my Lord!

UNBEKANNTES.

WARFARE.

"Ist genug für deinen Namen?"

Is Thy work all ended, Lord,
   For Thy servant here to do?
Shall I not go forth again,
   Meet my foes and Thine anew?
Shall I not, at Thy command,
   With Thy Word and Spirit's might,
Once again the conflict join,
   Raise Thy standard in the fight?

Many months have come and gone,
   Months of weariness and pain,
Since I laid my armour down,—
   Must I longer thus remain?
Must I tarry, useless, here,
   While around Thy foes combine?
Thou hast many stronger swords,
   None more willing, Lord, than mine!

Give me but the lowest place
  In Thy faithful, conquering band,
Let me prove what yet can do
  One devoted heart and hand!
Sorely wounded, faint, and weak,
  I was forced to leave the field;
But, Thou knowest, still this heart
  Fain would rather die than yield.

What though every danger past
  Were renewed tenfold again?
What although life's crimson tide
  Flowed afresh from every vein?
Lord, what hast Thou given for me?
  Hast Thou shrunk from pain or death?
In Thy service shall not I
  Gladly spend my latest breath?

From the field of battle won,
  All my toil and conflict o'er,
Let me hear Thy welcome call
  To Thyself for evermore!
With Thy banner o'er my head,
  Oh, what blessedness to die,—
Holy triumph, holy rest,
  In my latest look and sigh!

"Weeping, waiting, longing soul,
  Think not I despise thy prayer;
But—My sword thou well hast borne,
  Now My cross I bid thee bear."
Lord, Thy servant asks no more;
  Be it so, as Thou hast said;
Only, let Thy strength be now
  In my weakness perfect made!

Möwes.

JESUS ONLY.

"Saget mir von keinen Lieben."

TELL me not of earthly love,
Bid me not its sweetness prove,
If it do not heavenward tend,
And in Jesus find its end.

Tell me not of earthly bliss,
Bright, alluring as it is,
If its source I cannot see
In Thy love, my Lord, for me.

Tell me not of mental peace,
Till the sinner's conflicts cease;
Till that peace possess the heart
Jesus can alone impart.

Tell me not of knowledge high,
Roaming over earth and sky,—
This I know, worth all beside,
Jesus, and Him crucified.

JESUS ONLY.

Tell me not of earthly gain,—
Earthly pleasures to obtain;
I the priceless Pearl have found,—
I have all things, and abound.

Tell me not of earthly glory,
Wild ambition's wondrous story,—
Higher far my hopes can rise,
To a kingdom in the skies.

Tell me not of life below,
With its changing joy and woe;
Hid with God doth mine remain,
Life is Christ, and death is gain.

Not where death and change can come,
Is my portion or my home;
Jesus! all my bliss shall be
Sought and found alone in Thee!
UNBEKANNTES.

THE CROSS.

"Das Kreuz ist dennoch gut."

The Cross is ever good,
Although with tears bedewed;
A Father's hand from heaven
This very cross has given.
Take it, as children should:
   What bitter is at present,
   We own ere long as pleasant.
It is so good, so good!

The Cross is ever fair;
And though no beauty there
The eye of sight discerneth,
Such glory round it burneth,
That watching angels wear
   Sweet looks of joy and wonder,
   As on the Cross they ponder,
It is so fair, so fair!

And with the Cross is Light:
Before it nought aright
Of thine own self thou knowest,
While unto it thou owest,
Of God, the first true sight.
   The Cross in darkness finds thee,
     But scatters all that blinds thee ·
For with the Cross is Light.

The Cross makes all things pure:
No falsehood can endure
Its coming; guilt, long hidden,
Arises then unbidden;
And though severe the cure,
   At sorrow's touch must perish
     The sins we fain would cherish,
It makes so pure, so pure!

The Cross makes man so small,—
His proudest hopes must fall,
Their glory fast dispelling,
The while the Cross is telling
That God alone is All;
   That only He is holy,
     And must be worshipped solely,
Man is so small, so small!

The Cross to me is dear,—
It brings the Saviour near;
And, worldly joy resigning,
I take it unrepining.
Lord of the Cross! 'tis here
  My life, my all, I tender
  To Thee, in full surrender,
And thus the Cross is dear!

GERHARD TERSTEEGEN.

THE SONG OF SONGS.

"Es giebt ein Lied der Lieder."

THERE is a song now singing,—
Catch but its sweet beginning,
And you will still its notes prolong:
For ever, ever learning,
Yet never quite discerning
The deep, full meaning of the song!

It tells of love undying,
Before which grief is flying,
Like mists swept by the sun along.
Oh! how earth's sorrow leaveth
The heart that here receiveth
The holy music of the song!

SPITTA.

MORNING IN SPRING.

"Sieh, wie der Hain erwacht."

How nature wakes around!
  How the low rays of light
  Glitter in dew-drops bright!
What music in each sound;—
  Streams in their silver flow,
  Birds warbling clear and low,—
And now, behold the Monarch of the skies,
In his full glory, from his eastern couch arise!

How fresh this fragrant air!
  New life to all it brings,
  As if from hidden springs,
And I with nature share;
  Through every pulse I feel
  New life, new vigour steal:
O that my soul with yon light clouds could fly,
Above all beauty here, to its great Source on high!

Yes, all has come from Thee,
   Lord of all power and might!
   To chaos' silent night
Thou spakest—"Let there be!"
   And, answering to each name,
   Light, life, and beauty came.
And still the work of power does love maintain,
Revive, renew, through all Thy universal reign.

At length a morn shall come,
   When the last "Let there be!"
   Is spoken—and we see
This earth a glorious home,
   A temple, where no sin
   Nor death shall enter in,
Where Christ's redeemëd ones, serenely blest,
In the new heavens and earth for ever safe shall rest.

And now things fair and bright
   Are shadows, sent before,
   Of better things in store,
When these have sunk in night.
   Pass, shadows of to-day!
   Bright visions, fade away!
We mourn you not—let planets disappear,
When the red glowing east proclaims the Sun is near.

For me that Sun shall rise ;—
And loved ones, mourned in vain,
Its light shall bring again
To bless my longing eyes.
Then faint not, drooping heart,
Ours is the better part;
Bloom on, fair Nature! fading are thy flowers,
But things which perish not, in Christ are surely ours.

RUDOLPH STIER.

THE CALL OBEYED.

"O Ursprung des Lebens, O ewiges Licht."

O EVERLASTING Source of life and light,
Which none shall seek in vain who seeks aright,
  Fountain of love and peace,
  Here, in the wilderness,
Flowing, with living waters to impart
To every longing soul, to every weary heart,—

How sweetly sounds the call, Whoever will,
Let him draw near, secure of welcome still!
  Here mercy, full and free,
  Whate'er thy case may be,
Poor sinner, come in faith, and thou shalt find:
Rest for the burdened soul, balm for the wounded mind.

Lord, I am come; by faith I would abide,
With longing spirit, at the Fountain-side.
  Thou wilt not fail, nor break
  One promise Thou dost make,

To poor and needy souls. Thou wilt bestow
All that I need, for all Thou well must know.

How rich the treasures Jesus has to give !
How happy they who hear, believe, and live !
      All guilty fears will fly
        When He in love draws nigh.
Give me the blessing, Lord ; let each desire,
Now weaned from earth, to Thee and things of heaven
    aspire.

And should affliction come at Thy command,
Let me receive it meekly from Thy hand.
      Let me not start, nor shrink
        Of Thine own cup to drink ;
For they who share on earth Thy grief and pain,
Soon with Thyself in bliss for evermore shall reign.

Then, O my God, give me at length to rest,
Where all Thy people with Thyself are blest ;
      Where sin, and grief, and fear,
        For ever disappear ;
Where joy in all its fulness shall be given,
And all Love's toil on earth be overpaid in heaven.
C. J. KOITSCH.

SABBATH MORNING.

"Es wird mein Herz mit Freuden wach."

My heart wakes with a joyful lay:
There is a blessing on this day;
And many voices call abroad,
"O come and seek the House of God!"

To-day, when He will speak to thee,
Within His courts a waiter be;
To-day, thy busy hands be still,
And let Him work His blessed will.

God keeps an open house to-day,
The Bread of Life He gives away;
Each hungering soul He satisfies,
And he who eateth never dies.

To-day, the Sower broadcast sows
His precious seed where'er He goes;
And where preparëd hearts are found,
Like precious fruit will soon abound.

To-day, the faithful Shepherd leads
His little flock through flowery meads;
To quiet resting-places brings,
Green pastures, and fresh water-springs.

To-day, the great Physician comes -
Still nearer to our hearts and homes,
With loving counsel, and relief
For every wound, and pain, and grief.

A blessing rests upon this day :
My heart wakes with a joyful lay,
And gladly sounds the call abroad,—
" O come and seek the House of God ! "

SPITTA.

REMEMBER ME.

" Mein Gott, vergiss mein nicht."

My God, forget me not
   In sorrow's evil day,
When dark the shadows fall
   Around my pilgrim way.
To Thy sure word of hope
   Let me for refuge flee;
In mercy, then, for good,
   O Lord, remember me!

My God, forget me not,
   When low before Thy throne
I seek to spread my cares,
   And make my wishes known.
A Father's gracious face,
   By faith, then let me see;
I am Thy loving child,—
   O Lord, remember me!

My God, forget me not,
    When my poor soul is dumb,
And only sighs and tears,
    Instead of words, will come.
Though even sighs should cease,
    Desires are known to Thee;—
In pity, then, and love,
    O Lord, remember me!

My God, forget me not,
    When all around is bright;
Undazzled let me walk
    Amid the sunshine light.
Give me a quiet mind,
    From earthly bondage free;
Be Thou my chiefest joy,—
    O Lord, remember me!

My God, forget me not,
    When this forgetful heart
Is tempted, from Thy ways
    To wander and depart;
Give me to find no rest
    Till I return to Thee,
In lowly penitence,—
    O Lord, remember me!

My God, forget me not,
　When my last hour is near,
And all the things of earth
　Grow dim or disappear.
Through the dark valley's shade
　Thy glory let me see;
My light in life, in death,—
　O Lord, remember me!

WILHELM VON BIANOWSKY.

PEACE.

"Gib deinen Frieden uns, O Herr der Starke!"

Give us Thy blessed peace, God of all might!
Without it, we must weary in the fight;
Without it, our weak service soon must cease:
    Give us Thy blessed peace.

Life's day is sultry, and its evening chill,
With little left to cheer; yet the heart still
Cleaveth to dust, nor can obtain release,
    Excepting through Thy peace.

Lord, give us peace, let it refresh anew
The deeply tempted, yet the tried and true,
Lest evil spirits foil us in the strife
    Of this too earnest life.

The fathers, loved by Thee, this blessing knew:
Their children in the desert need it too.
Give peace, and hope to lay our weapons down,
    And gain the victor's crown.

Our life below, until the journey close,
Is often stormy, and beset with foes:
Lord, in the shadow of Thy peace give rest,
  When we are most opprest.

And whensoever death itself appear,
Then may Thy angel messengers be near,
And bear us hence, to share, when troubles cease,
  Thine everlasting peace!

C. B. GARVE.

WALKING IN LIGHT.

"Wenn wir uns kindlich freuen."

When we seek, with loving heart,
Each to act a childlike part,
Daily duty, daily care,
For our Lord to do or bear,—

All His pleasure to fulfil,
Do or suffer all His will;
Serve Him here with earnest love,
Till we dwell with Him above,—

When the ransomed look before,
View by faith the heavenly shore,
Catch the echoes of the song
They shall join in there, ere long,—

Then, of small account appear
Every mortal toil or tear;
Homeward hasting day by day,
What are trials by the way?

WALKING IN LIGHT.

He, the great High Priest, draws nigh,
Brings for every want supply;
Healing oil, and cheering wine,
Living water, bread divine.

Then together all rejoice,
Singing praise with heart and voice;
Finding, ere our work be done,
Present heaven on earth begun.

Often by our Saviour blest
With a sweet sabbatic rest,
Every burden we can bear
To His heart, and leave it there.

And arising, onward haste,
When that blessed hour is past;
Ready, with uplifted hands,
For the Master's next commands.

Ready, at His midnight call,
Joyfully to part from all—
Then, with Him, the festal door
Enter, to go out no more!

MORAVIAN.

FUNERAL HYMN.

"Ehmalls sollt gestorben seyn."

Once the sentence justly sounded,
  "Thou shalt die!" in accents dread,
To the erring sheep, who wandered
  In forbidden paths to tread;
But how awfully it lighted
  On the Shepherd's sinless head!

And since *He* endured that anguish,
  Bore those sorrows, deep and vast,
For His people, death is altered,
  All its bitterness is past;
As they journey where He leads them,
  'Tis a step, and that the last.

So from time to time the Master
  Calleth home His servants still,
One by one, the many mansions
  In His Father's house to fill.

Shall we dare His love to question,
   Or dispute His sovereign will?

Go in peace, beloved brother!
   At the call of Jesus go,
To behold Him in His beauty,
   All His love and grace to know.
Thou departest,—we must linger
   In the land of sin and woe.

Rest in peace—the rest is pleasant,
   When our toil and strife are o'er;
All the sweeter for the conflict
   Or the weariness before;—
Thou hast laboured long and nobly,
   Thou shalt rest for evermore!

While thy memory we cherish,
   Ever honoured, ever dear,
Till we meet again, when Jesus
   Shall have banished every tear,
And with rapture, reunited,
   All thy tale of glory hear!

                       COUNT ZINZENDORF.

LIGHT IN DARKNESS.

"Frühlingluft, um blaue Berge spielend."

BREEZES of spring, all earth to life awaking,—
    Birds swiftly soaring through the sunny sky,—
The butterfly its lonely prison breaking,—
    The seed upspringing, which had seemed to die,—

Types such as these a word of hope have spoken,
    Have shed a gleam of light around the tomb;
But weary hearts longed for a surer token,
    A clearer ray, to dissipate its gloom.

And this was granted! See the Lord ascending,
    On crimson clouds of evening calmly borne,
With hands outstretched, and looks of love still bending
    On His bereaved ones, who no longer mourn.

"I am the resurrection," hear Him saying,
    "I am the life; he who believes in Me

Shall never die,—the souls My call obeying,
 Soon, where I am, for evermore shall be."

Sing Hallelujah! light from heaven appearing,
 The mystery of life and death is plain;
Now to the grave we can descend unfearing,
 In sure and certain hope to rise again!

Unbekanntes.

CHRISTMAS HYMN.

" Dies ist der Tag."

" This is the day the Lord hath made,"
O'er all the earth let this be said.
Praise Him for all the mercies given
Through Jesus Christ in earth and heaven.

The nations longed, through ages past,—
The time appointed came at last;
Then the great Father sent the Son,
Immanuel, the Holy One.

Oh! when this miracle of grace
I seek to ponder, deep amaze
Comes o'er me, and I only see
How passing thought its marvels be!

Rejoice, ye heavens; be glad, O earth,
On this blest day of Jesu's birth!
Above, below, let all combine
In the new song of love divine!

Ch. Gellert.

REDEEMING LOVE.

"Jesu, meines Leben's Leben."

Thou eternal life bestowest,
  Thou hast death as victor slain;
Thou hast bowed in deepest anguish,
  Bodily and mental pain,
Us poor sinners to deliver,
Save from sin and death for ever,—
  Thanks, a thousand thanks to Thee,
  Saviour, for Thy love so free!

O Thou Son of God most holy,
  Thou hast borne reproach and shame,
Cruel blows and bitter mocking,
  Every vile and scornful name;
Bonds and stripes so meekly taking,
Thus our chains and fetters breaking,—
  Thanks, a thousand thanks to Thee,
  Saviour, for Thy love so free!

Oh, so deeply Thou wast wounded,
  That our wounds might all be whole;
Thou didst labour, worn and weary,
  Rest to give each weary soul.
Yea, the very curse enduredst,
Blessing then for us securedst;—
  Thanks, a thousand thanks to Thee,
  Saviour, for Thy love so free!

Now with glowing heart we bless Thee
  For each hour of pain and gloom;
For the mocking hall of judgment,
  For the cross and for the tomb,
For Thy groaning and Thy sighing,
For Thy bleeding and Thy dying:
  Thanks, eternal thanks to Thee,
  For Thy love so rich and free!

E. C. Homburg.

THE PRINCE OF LIFE.

"Christ lag in Todesbanden."

Jesus in bonds of death had lain,
   For our offences dying;
But now the Lord is risen again,
   And Death is vanquished lying.
Thus believers can rejoice,
Give praise and thanks with cheerful voice,
   Loud hallelujahs singing!
              Hallelujah!

That was a strange and awful strife,
   When Life with Death contended;
The Victor was the Prince of Life,
   Who Death's dominion ended.
Thus the promise is made plain,
Jesus by dying Death has slain;
   We dread our foe no longer.
              Hallelujah!

Then let us join to keep the feast
   In holy love and gladness;
With Jesus enter into rest,
   Set free from fear and sadness.
He's the Sun whose radiance bright
Has filled our hearts with joyful light;
   The darkness now is over!
                Hallelujah!

LUTHER.

PRAYER AND SUPPLICATION.

"O Gott, du frommer Gott."

O GREAT and gracious God,
   Of every good the Giver,
Creating all at first,
   Upholding all for ever!
Grant me a body free
   From sad disease or pain,—
A soul from sin redeemed,
   A conscience without stain.

What Thou dost call to do
   Let me be ever doing,
The task Thou shalt appoint
   With diligence pursuing;
Teach me the time, the way,
   Thy purpose to fulfil,
And then the blessing give,—
   So shall I prosper still.

When dangers rise around,
  Then keep me from despairing,
With holy courage filled,
  The cross in patience bearing.
By gentleness and love
  May I each foe subdue,
And find in time of need
  True friends and counsel true.

Let me, when death is nigh,
  Remember Jesus dying,
And so in peace depart,
  On His sure love relying.
Then may my soul with joy
  Before Thy face appear,
And grant my dust a grave
  Beside Thy people here.

And on that solemn day,
  When all the dead are waking,
Stretch o'er my grave Thy hand,
  Its gates and barriers breaking.
Then shall I hear Thy voice,
  These eyes my Saviour see,
And soul and body dwell
  In bliss at home with Thee!

J. Heermann.

SACRAMENTAL HYMN.

"Schmücke dich, o liebe Seele."

Soul, arise, dispel thy sadness,
Hear the voice of hope and gladness;
Gloomy shades of sin forsaking,
Come, where morning light is breaking.
Hear the gracious invitation
From the God of thy salvation,
He, the God of heaven, presiding,
For His sinful guest providing.

Oh! my heart is longing, sighing,
For this feast of Love's supplying!
Longing that the bread of heaven
To my fainting soul were given,—
That my Lord were life bestowing
From His cup of love o'erflowing,—
Thirsting for a living union
With Himself, in blest communion.

SACRAMENTAL HYMN.

Help me, Lord, Thy goodness tasting,
On the sacred symbols feasting,
Not in vain Thy grace receiving,
Not unworthy, unbelieving,
But with lowly faith desiring,
More and more Thy love admiring,—
Till Thy welcome call is given
To the marriage-feast in heaven!

Joh. Franck.

THINGS NEW AND OLD.

"Zum neuen Jahr den alten Vater."

With the New Year the old, sure Refuge still,
   Our Father ruling on His throne above!
He guides the nations by His sovereign will,
   He bears His people on His wings of love.
Thy gracious care through all the past we see,
The unknown future we can leave with Thee!

With the New Year grant a new blessing, Lord!
   Still unexhausted is Thy bounteous hand;
Roses shall blossom, if Thou giv'st the word,
   And fountains murmur, in the desert land.
Thy blessing fills the basket and the store;
Give as Thou seest good—we ask no more.

With the New Year old burdens still of care—
   The year of jubilee is not yet come;
Still must we nerve our hearts, to do or bear,
   Pilgrims and strangers on the journey home.

Not here our rest—to trial yet and toil
We must go forward, through life's "little while."

With the New Year new hopes, for earth and heaven!
    Fair Nature's summer beauties shall return,
And to us also sunshine shall be given—
    Our Father's children do not always mourn;
New gifts of love Hope in the future sees,
And far beyond them "greater things than these."

With the New Year may the old faith remain!
    Rise, soldiers of the Cross, to fight once more!
Let the old standard be unfurled again—
    "In this we conquer" now, as oft of yore!
Still the old battle-cry, the old broad shield—
Christ and His host again shall keep the field!

With the New Year renew our hearts, O God!
    Renew our strength, to run the heavenly way;
In the old paths, where all Thy saints have trod,
    O Saviour, lead us! help us, day by day,
Through storm or calm, our journey to pursue,
Till the bright morn when all shall be made new!

CARL GEROK.

ALPINE LYRICS.

Translator's Preface.

THE name of Meta Heusser, *née* Schweizer, is perhaps not generally known in England, though so dear to the lovers of sanctified genius and sacred song in her native Switzerland, and Germany. Pastor Knapp, editor of the "Liederschatz" (the most extensive collection of German hymns), himself a talented poet, was first to discover the genius of the Swiss lady, and to draw her, reluctantly, from her modest retirement. In the third edition of his "Liederschatz," he says of her:—"An admirable writer, whose tender, spiritual lays far surpass those of former German poetesses." And in the first published collection of her poems he writes in the preface:—"She knows alike how to breathe the flute-like tones (Flötenton) of faith, or to sound its trumpet-call among the children of God."

Dr. Koch, in his "Geschichte des Kirchenlieds," third edition, says:—"From contemplation of the glorious Alpine world, and the atmosphere of spiritual freedom which she daily and hourly breathes out of the Sacred Scriptures, have sprung the tender yet deeply reflective poems which have made her, Meta Heusser, the most eminent and noble among all the female poets of our whole Evangelical Church. Her lays flow freely from the fresh fountain of a heart in constant, holy communion with God."

Dr. Philip Schaff of New York, editor of the beautiful collection, "Christ in Song," justly proud of his honoured countrywoman and life-long friend, calls her in his own work "the most gifted and sweetest of female poets in the German tongue;" and in a late letter to myself, he writes of "the characteristics of her poems, as combining true poetic genius with deep piety, and experience in the school of affliction, which impart to them an air of holy sadness and home-longings after heaven," and thus render them peculiarly attractive and consoling for sad and bereaved hearts.

It has been no small pleasure for myself to comply with the earnest request of Dr. Schaff, and prepare for the press this small selection of translations from the poems of the gifted, venerable lady, whom I have the happiness to call a personal friend. It is now many long years since I first felt the charm of her genius, discovering her hymns as perfect gems in the "Liederschatz," though knowing nothing then of the writer's personal history. Some of the present translations will be recognized as having appeared already in "Hymns from the Land of Luther" and "Thoughtful Hours;" but the greater number are quite new.

I am well aware that my pleasant task is but imperfectly executed. The depth of feeling in Meta Heusser's poems, her perfect mastery over her native language, and the richness of her imagery, combined with condensation of thought, make her a most difficult author to render into English verse. This, I believe, any one will acknowledge who has made the attempt.

In various instances I have found it impossible, for my own satisfaction, to give other than a free version, preserving in our language the general ideas and spirit of the original. In other cases I have reluctantly, for the present at least, laid aside some of those pieces which I specially admired. Finding that the Easter Hymn, page 293, had been already translated, at Dr. Schaff's request, by Professor T. C. Porter of Lafayette College, and despairing of myself doing equal justice to this very fine but difficult poem, I gratefully accepted permission to reprint it from "Christ in Song."

Yet, notwithstanding the imperfections which I so readily acknowledge, I believe the specimens here given from the writings of my honoured friend will find an echo and a welcome in many Christian hearts, especially from such readers as are ignorant of or imperfectly acquainted with the German language. Others, more fortunate, will gladly turn to seek for themselves the higher enjoyment of studying the beautiful, unalloyed originals.

An accomplished daughter of the poetess has most kindly written for this volume a graceful sketch of her mother's history, of which the following is a translation:—

"The Swiss poetess, Meta Heusser, *née* Schweizer, some of whose writings have now become accessible to English readers through the medium of translation, was born April 6th, 1797, as the fourth daughter of Pastor Diethelm Schweizer, in the little mountain village of Hirzel, canton Zurich. She grew up in this quiet retirement, with few means of instruction, excepting the Book of Books and the Book of Nature. Both of these she studied diligently; and the deep insight which she obtained into both was afterwards very clearly shown in her poems.

"The poetic inspiration early touched her soul, and she could not choose but sing, 'as the bird sings among the branches.' Great, therefore, must her joy have been when Goethe's and Schiller's works found their way into the solitary parsonage. Sitting at her spinning-wheel, along with her sisters, she learned with enthusiasm many of Schiller's ballads, and soon making acquaintance with other authors, her memory became a rich treasury of song, secular and sacred, which remains her own even in old age, each passing event recalling some appropriate quotation.

"Although her gifted mind seemed formed to influence a large circle, God had determined otherwise, and her sphere of labour was to be a narrow one. 'My thoughts are not your thoughts, neither are your ways my ways, saith the Lord.'

"In the year 1821 she married Dr. Heusser, a talented, excellent physician, who had settled in Hirzel, to the great consolation of all sufferers in that neighbourhood, who previously had to send to a distance for medical aid. Henceforward we may apply to our poetess the words of Chamisso,—

'Hers was woman's usual lot,
Cares and trials wanting not.'

Children were born and brought up. She had seven—three sons and four daughters—of whom one son has gone before her to the eternal world. There were also a multitude of household and other duties to be fulfilled, including attention to her husband's patients, several of whom were always resident in the house. All the prosaic burdens of common life came upon her; yet her poetic genius, far from sinking under them, soared above all, as the palm-tree is said to grow best under weights. She now sang more than ever; but for her own enjoyment only, little dreaming that her lays would ever be given to the world.

"Her friends, however, thought differently. Knapp, in Stuttgart, was the first person who obtained permission to make public some of her 'spirit-children,' and in the year 1834 several of her poems for the first time appeared in print, under the name of 'Einer Verborgenen' (a hidden one), in Knapp's Almanack, 'Christoterpe.'

"From this time forward her poems appeared in various other collections, and were widely circulated. In 1855 Knapp visited the poetess, with the view of persuading her to allow the publication of her writings as a separate volume. He came *resolved* to gain his object, and did succeed at last; but only after long resistance, for 'Die Verborgene' was most unwilling to leave her retirement.

"Two years after this visit, the first volume of her poems appeared, and in 1867 a second followed. What she had sung in her quiet chamber, to relieve her own full heart, has now become a common treasure, not for German readers alone, but for English ones also,—thanks to the efforts of her friend, Dr. Schaff of New York, and to the translator of 'Hymns from the Land of Luther.'

"But we must return to the sketch of her life-story. In 1859 Meta Heusser became a widow. Her husband, considerably older than herself, worn out by many labours, grew weaker day by day; but she had the joy of seeing that while his bodily strength failed his spiritual life developed, and in the full sense of the words he 'went home' at last to the Lord. Since then she has dwelt with her only surviving sister, who has been her life-long companion and good angel,* and with her two youngest daughters; her other children having married and dispersed far and near.

"On the free heights of the Hirzel, looking round upon the mountain ranges, and the blue lakes of Zurich and Zug, the poetess has passed her whole life; and here she will still dwell, until at last, weary, as she often says, with her lengthened pilgrimage, she shall leave her beautiful earthly home for that other, yet more beautiful, for which she so often longs. 'Happy they who feel the home-sickness,—they are on the way to home.'"

H. L. L.

* Since the above was written, the venerable lady and her sister have both been called to the heavenly rest. Meta Heusser departed in peace, deeply loved and lamented, on January 2, 1876. Fräulein Schweizer had died in the autumn of 1874.

ALPINE LYRICS.

MOUNTAINS.

"The everlasting hills!" how calm they rise,
    Bold witnesses to an Almighty Hand!
We gaze with longing heart and eager eyes,
And feel as if short pathway might suffice
    From those pure regions to the heavenly land.

At early dawn, when the first rays of light
    Play like a rose-wreath on the peaks of snow;
And late, when half the valley seems in night,
Yet still around each pale majestic height
    The sun's last smile has left a crimson glow;—

Then the heart longs, it calls for wings to fly,—
    Above all lower scenes of earth to soar,
Where yonder golden clouds arrested lie,

Where granite cliffs and glaciers gleam on high
    As with reflected light from Heaven's own door.

Whence this strange spell, by thoughtful souls confest
    Ever in shadow of the mountains found?
'Tis the deep voice within our human breast,
Which bids us seek a refuge and a rest
    Above, beyond what meets us here around!

Ever to men of God the hills were dear,
    Since on the slopes of Ararat the dove
Plucked the wet olive-pledge of hope and cheer;
Or Israel stood entranced in silent fear,
    While God on Sinai thundered from above......

And once on Tabor was a vision given
    Sublime as that which Israel feared to view,
When the transfigured Lord of earth and heaven,
Mortality's dim curtain lifted, riven,
    Revealed His glory to His chosen few.

On mountain heights of Galilee He prayed,
    While others slept, and all beneath was still;
From Olivet's recess of awful shade
Thrice was that agonized petition made,
    "O that this cup might pass, if such Thy will!"......

And on Mount Zion, in the better land,
    Past every danger of the pilgrim way,
At our Redeemer's feet we hope to stand,
And learn the meanings of His guiding hand
    Through all the changes of our earthly day.

Then hail, calm sentinels of heaven, again!
    Proclaim your message, as in ages past!
Tell us that pilgrims shall not toil in vain,
That Zion's mount we surely shall attain,
    Where all home longings find a home at last!

UNDER THE STARS.

  Stars of the silent night,
  Moving in golden light
So calmly through the vault above!
  Could I but follow you,
  And my life-course pursue
Shedding all round me light and love!

  But comes the crushing thought—
  I am a thing of nought,
I seem so feeble, worthless, small;
  Who thinks of care or grief
  For a pale autumn leaf,
When he beholds it fade and fall?

  Why do these longings vain
  Ever return again?
Why should my weak and wayward soul
  Strive in her narrow grasp
  Eternity to clasp,
And the Almighty Ruler of the whole?

O Thou Unseen, Divine!
I long to find Thee mine,
But all my search and labours fail;—
And to my yearning cry
Fair Nature makes reply
With echoes sad, from hill and vale.

Is it an angel's voice
Bidding my soul rejoice?
My weary heart has heard of One,
Whose unexampled love
Led Him, in heaven above,
To leave for earth His glory-throne.

Wearing the humble veil
Of manhood weak and frail,
The lowly paths of earth He trod;
Yet would a light divine
Through all His actions shine,
The Son of man, yet Son of God.

Our fallen race to save,
His own life-blood He gave,
Dying in agony and shame;—
And now, set free from fear,
The sinner may draw near
To the great God, in Jesus' name.

My longing eyes I raise—
Ah, I can bear to gaze
On this mild Form of Majesty!
In Him I dare to trust;
On me, low in the dust,
I feel He looks with pitying eye.

And of this blissful faith,
This hope for life and death,
Philosophy would rob my hold!
You strike his staff away,
And reach no better stay
To the blind wanderer on the wold!

What comfort can you boast
To give, when mine is lost,
From your own cold and shadowy creed?
Not such as Christ imparts
To lonely, breaking hearts,
Crying to Him for help in need.

To rebel thought and will
He whispers, "Peace, be still!"
Leading the way to home and rest:
For every cross and care
Gives strength to do or bear,—
In joy or sorrow, I am blest!

And in this vale of tears,
Of nameless doubts and fears,
Errors and falls on every side,
Shall my soul turn away
From the celestial ray
Of Light from heaven, my Hope, my Guide?

Ah no! this loving One,
Sinless Himself alone,
Whose life for sinners once was given,
Who journeyed through the grave,
The lost to seek and save—
He is my God, for earth and heaven!

AT MIDNIGHT.

BESIDE MY SLEEPING CHILDREN.

Darkness reigns—the hum of life's commotion
   On the listening ear no longer breaks;
Stars are shining on the deep blue ocean;
   All is silent—Love alone awakes.

Love on earth her lonely vigil keeping,
   Love in heaven that rests or slumbers not,—
Peace, my anxious heart! though thou wert sleeping
   Love Divine has ne'er its charge forgot.

And for you, my brightest earthly flowers,
   You, my children, Love Divine has cared;
Sleep, beloved ones! through these dark hours
   Angels by your pillow watch and guard.

Here the wingèd messengers of Heaven,
   As beheld at Bethel, come and go;

AT MIDNIGHT.

Angel guardians, whom the Lord has given
    To each little one while here below.

Do I feel their pinions, gently waving?
    Are they watching me, too, from above?
Ah! my faith looks higher, humbly craving
    Blessings greater far than angel-love.

Thou, O Saviour, when on earth residing,
    Never didst Thou scorn a mother's prayer;
Faith may still behold Thee here abiding,
    Still commend her treasures to Thy care.

Thine they are,—from Thee did I receive them,—
    See, again I lay them on Thy breast;
Never may the Tempter's art deceive them,—
    Make them in Thyself for ever blest!

Were not all my hope on Thee reposing,
    Thou sole refuge for a sinner's fears,
Then, the future all its ills disclosing,
    I could give my children only tears.

From their earthly parents they inherit
    Only sin and weakness, grief and pain;
Give them, Lord, Thine all-sufficient merit,
    Spiritual birth and life again.

Give them the new name, and safely write them
    In Thy book, to share Thy children's lot;
Earth may separate—do Thou unite them
    In the bonds which Death dissolveth not.

By Thy rod and staff in mercy lead them
    In the footsteps of Thy flock below,
Till 'mid heavenly pastures Thou shalt feed them
    Where the streams of life eternal flow.

Sleep, my darlings, in the Shepherd's keeping!
    Peace, my heart! His promise stands for aye!
Swift it flies, our night of toil and weeping,
    Soon shall dawn the everlasting day!

THEODORA.

(1822.)

I MUST go hence,—here there is nought abiding,—
   My eyes have gazed and questioned all around;
In all the charms of earth no lasting portion,
   No home for me, no resting-place I found.

I must go hence,—the pale night violet closes
   Its fragrant petals at the dawn of day,—
The nightingale is silent,—through the valley
   The streamlet to the ocean hastes away;—

I too must go,—my trial-days are over;
   Where I am going there is no more pain;
No cold, rude grasp, shall crush the heart's affection,
   The wounds of earth shall all be healed again.

I must go hence,—while others joy in spring-time,
   The early autumn of my life has come;
The early ripe must be the early gathered,—
   Come, reaper-angels, bear me safely home!

Yes, I go home;—on my brief pilgrim journey
    No bridal wreath for me let Love prepare;
Yet in the distance I behold one gleaming,—
    A wreath of amaranth, more pure and fair!

I must go home,—why are ye sadly weeping?
    I was not made for toil and conflict; why
Should your true hearts, kind friends, be sad and troubled,
    Because a drooping flower must fade and die?

I must go home,—a strange and lonely journey,
    Through Death's dark valley; but I see afar
Beyond the gloom, a beacon light is shining,
    The guiding rays of Mercy's morning star.

I must go home,—O Saviour! Thou hast spoken
    Peace to my heart; I come at Thy command!
Thou too hast died; but Thou hast life eternal,
    And my soul's life is safe within Thy hand.

The hour has come,—oh, I am weary, weary!
    Are there not angel-voices in the air?
Heaven's gates unfold, in peace my eyes are closing;
    I shall awake in joy and safety there!

ALONE AT EVENING.

Weary and sad I stray,
While the last lights of day
  Fade in the western sky.

Dear ones are distant far;
Yonder bright evening star
  Hears not my lonely sigh.

Music and smiles all round,
Love and delights I found,
  Making *my* heart more lone;

Solitude suits with grief,—
None can bring mine relief
  Who has not sorrow known.

Does not a Form appear
Known to my soul, and dear,
  Loving, and calm, and sad?

Couldst thou forget *Him* so,
Long since acquainted with woe,
   Making the mourners glad?

Lowly to earth He came,
Bearing our sin and shame,
   Learning our grief and pain:

Gently His love imparts
Comfort to broken hearts,
   Bidding them hope again.

Now I despond no more;
Darkness and doubt are o'er,
   Love everlasting mine!

Yonder bright evening star
Joins me from heaven afar,
   Praising this Friend Divine!

TO MY YOUNGEST CHILD,

ON HER CONFIRMATION DAY.

Whence comes that mournful look and sigh,
   Dear child, as though this sacred day
Were but a time of sad farewells,
   Not of new welcomes on thy way?

Thou mournest childhood's vanished joys?
   Ah, love, thy mother feels with thee!
For her the latest buds of spring
   Fade with thy childhood's closing glee.

Yet where one Eden disappears,
   Another smiles to soothe our loss;
The flowers of everlasting spring
   Bloom in the shadow of the Cross.

And Faith can hear a Father's voice,
   Eternal Love, in accents mild,

Call to each lonely, troubled heart,—
"Come home, and be my joyful child!"

Still art thou troubled and cast down?
Still I can hear a gentle sigh:
"Yes, there *are* treasures others find,
But oh, how weak and poor am I!"

Oh, well for thee, my love, as now,
To feel thy weakness and thy woe;
How shall the sick one seek a cure,
Who has not learned his need to know?

Come, then, my child, and dry thy tears,
For us the Saviour's once were shed;
And now no heart need long in vain,
No mourner weep uncomforted.

Take comfort then, Christ calleth thee!
He bids thee seek Him *as thou art;*—
Come with thy poverty and pain,
Lay at His feet thine empty heart.

He calls thee to His feast of love,
Where still, as in the ages past,
His people find a port of rest,
A shelter from life's stormy blast.

And if the gate seem sealed for thee
    Where deepest mysteries are stored,
And heights of love and joy unknown,
    Which others share around that board,—

Yet none the less, in humble trust,
    Take thou the holy bread and wine;
So, peacefully, a slumbering babe
    Receives another sacred sign.

Doubt not the Saviour lives for thee;
    Believe, and hope, and trust, and rest,
Till the Dove brings the olive branch
    Of perfect peace to make thee blest.

The Shepherd's hand shall feed *thee* still,
    When long thy mother's toils are o'er,
Till by the living streams above
    We meet in joy, to part no more.

He calleth all His flock by name—
    Thy name is not forgotten then.
So be it, Lord! guard her and bless,
    Now, evermore! Amen! Amen!

TO A NAME-CHILD BEYOND THE SEA.

CHILD, dear child! though to divide us
   Seas and continents combine,
Yet by bonds of faithful friendship,
   And thy name, I call thee mine!

Mighty barriers of nature
   Hopeless rise between us here;
Never may our living voices
   Hold communion close and dear.

These few lines, Affection's greeting,
   Ne'er, perchance, may meet thine eyes;
Yet the shadow proves the substance,—
   Love shall live when Nature dies.

Long before our land and ocean
   Rose from chaos into day,
Long ere man had sinned and sorrowed,
   Love Eternal held its sway.

Then the Book of Life was open,
    And within its pages fair
Many a name had Love recorded,—
    Thine and mine, I trust, are there!

And that Love Divine, Eternal,
    Still shall reign unchanging on,
When our time and space have vanished,
    With the old Earth past and gone.

In His name of Love, who, dying,
    God and man hath reconciled;
In His name, the True and Faithful,
    I would bless thee, precious child!

In thy soul, a watered garden,
    From thy childhood's early days
May the plants of Eden flourish,
    To the heavenly Gardener's praise.

Every holy, varied blessing,
    By thy godly fathers known,
May the daughter now inherit,
    Claim and manifest her own!

Thou, a pilgrim here and stranger,
    Like thy fathers all below,

To the Everlasting City
   Through the vale of tears must go.

But may He, who little children
   Loved, and folded to His breast,
Guard from ill thine infant weakness,
   Give thy youthful spirit rest.

On Him all thy hopes be centred,
   In His strength thy life-work done;
East and west He hath united,—
   Heaven and Earth in Him are one!

DAVID AND JONATHAN.

True, brother friends! whose depth of love
Their own sad hearts best learned to prove
    In time of anguish sore!
Through the long centuries since then,
How oft that grief has come again,—
    Parting to meet no more!

By strange, mysterious guidance led,
What varied paths these two should tread,
    To death, and to a crown!
David the royal throne ascends—
On the lost battle-field his friend
    Low in his blood lies down.

Long have the echoes died away
Of that sad elegiac lay,
    Sung by the mourning king;
And silent, too, each joyful song,
Which of glad worshippers the throng
    In Zion used to sing.

All long, long silent! but the word
Of David's Son and David's Lord
    Reveals a better land,
Where, free from sin, and grief, and fears,
The friends who parted once in tears
    Together crownëd stand.

True love in Christ is never vain,—
Who gave it first, restores again,
    When parting griefs are past.
Far-severed streams, in murmurs sweet,
Tell of the ocean where they meet
    In endless peace at last.

THE BROOK.*

Fair stream of the peaceful valley,
　　Murmuring soft and low,
Have they robbed thee of all thy treasures,
　　That thou art wailing so?

Ah! what pictures of perfect beauty
　　Once in thy calm mirror slept!—
The graceful birches and alders,
　　The willow that waved and wept,—

The cool, deep-shaded places,
　　Where the wild-fowl loved to rest,—
The squirrel among the branches,
　　The linnet low in her nest!

But the sound of axe and hatchet
　　Came down the quiet dell;

* Free translation.

Then the birch and the alder vanished,
    The willow sighed and fell.

Now all is bare and dreary;—
    Over the cold gray stone
Thou goest, mourning and seeking
    For loved companions gone.

Yet see!—the blue heaven is mirrored
    There, where the shadows lay;
The moon and the stars at midnight,
    The glorious sun by day.

Flow on thy course to the ocean,
    Fair stream, and lament no more!
Thou hast gained more abiding treasures
    Than all those possessed before.

I, too, may pursue my journey,
    And lament not nor repine,—
What matter though Earth be lonely,
    If Heaven at last be mine!

EASTER HYMN.*

Lamb, the once crucified! Lion, by triumph surrounded!
Victim all bloody, and Hero, who hell hast confounded!
    Pain-riven Heart,
      That from earth's deadliest smart
Over the heavens hast bounded!

Thou in the depths wert to mortals the highest revealing;
God in humanity veiled, Thy full glory concealing!
    "Worthy art Thou!"
      Shouteth eternity now,
Praise to Thee endlessly pealing.

Heavenly Love, in the language of earth past expression!
Lord of all worlds, unto whom every tongue owes confession!

* Translated by Professor T. C. Porter, of Lafayette College. Reprinted, by permission, from "Christ in Song."

Didst Thou not go,
And, under sentence of woe,
Rescue the doomed by transgression?

O'er the abyss of the grave, and its horrors infernal,
Victory's palm Thou art waving in triumph supernal:
Who to Thee cling,
Circled by hope, shall now bring
Out of its gulf hope eternal.

Son of man, Saviour, in whom, with deep tenderness blending,
Infinite Pity to wretches her balm is extending;
On Thy dear breast,
Weary and numb, they may rest,
Quickened to joy never-ending.

Strange condescension! Immaculate Purity deigning
Union with souls where the vilest pollution was reigning;
Beareth their sin,
Seeketh the fallen to win;
Even the lowest regaining.

Sweetly persuasive, to me, too, Thy call has resounded;
Melting my heart so obdurate, Thy love has abounded:

EASTER HYMN.

      Back to the fold,
      Led by Thy hand, I behold
Grace all my path has surrounded.

Bless thou the Lord, O my soul! who, thy pardon assuring,
Heals thy diseases, and grants thee new life everduring;
      Joy amid woe,
      Peace amid strife here below,
Unto thee ever securing.

Upward, on pinions celestial, to regions of pleasure,
Into the land whose bright glories no mortal can measure,
      Strong hope and love
      Bear thee, the fulness to prove
Of thy salvation's rich treasure.

There, as He is, we shall view Him, with rapture abiding;
Cheered even here by His glance, when the darkness dividing
      Lets down a ray
      Over the perilous way,
Thousands of wanderers guiding.

Join, O my voice, the vast chorus, with trembling
    emotion,—
Chorus of saints, who, though sundered by land and by
    ocean,
        With sweet accord
        Praise the same glorious Lord,—
One in their ceaseless devotion.

Break forth, O Nature, in song, when the spring-tide is
    nighest!
World that hast seen His salvation, no longer thou
    sighest!
        Shout, starry train,
        From your empyreal plain,
"Glory to God in the highest!"

PILGRIM SONG.

A FEW more conflicts, toils, and tears,
A little more of griefs and fears—
The seed of hope for joys to come:
Love, as a gentle friend and guide,
Walks by the faithful pilgrim's side,
And soothes his sorrows, on the journey home.

Sweeter than words of mortal love,
We hear the message from above,
By ransomed souls in glory sung:
"Now all our tears are wiped away,
While Jesus leads us, day by day,
The trees of life and living streams among."

The shades of evening hasten on,
The summer heats will soon be gone;
Short, at the longest, is our road;
Hark! every hour, with passing-bell,
Seems of that coming hour to tell
Which brings us to our Father's blest abode.

And every pilgrim, who has passed
Through all our trials, safe at last,
Leaves a bright track along the way
To the fair City, where each guest
Is welcomed to the bridal feast,
By the great King, whom all in love obey.

How bright the dear ones gone before,
Beside the Lord for evermore,
Now to the eye of Faith appear!
Let feeble knees and hearts be strong :—
Forward! the toil will not be long,
For victory, and rest, and home are near!

PILGRIM PRAYERS.

Thou hast borne our sins and sorrows,
   Son of man, Thyself alone!
Look upon Thy pilgrim people
   Now, from Thine exalted throne!

In Thy tender love and mercy,
   Watch, O Lord, Thy little band;
Shed upon us, as we journey,
   Wondrous blessings from Thy hand.

Let Thy Spirit's gentle breathing
   Fan and foster life divine,
Till we tread with firmer footsteps
   In this narrow way of Thine.

Let each soul Thy words of blessing—
   " Peace be with you!"—gladly hear.
In each hour of toil or sorrow
   May Thy love our spirits cheer.

When our wayward hearts would wander,
    Lead and keep us in Thy ways;
Let a Sabbath rest refresh us
    After toilsome, weary days.

When temptations press around us,
    When our strength is fain to yield,
Let us see Thee, and take courage;
    Be our Captain, Shelter, Shield!

When the midnight shadows darken,
    Let the Morning Star appear;
On the wings of meek devotion
    May we rise, and find Thee near.

When the lamp of faith is failing,
    Lord, the oil of grace supply;
To the Canaan of our promise
    Make us look with clearer eye.

In each heart, with love and blessing,
    Saviour, let Thy kingdom come;
And in closest bonds united,
    Lead us to our Father's home.

O how full, how sweet a chorus,
    Shall proclaim Thy power and love,
When the pilgrims all are gathered
    In Jerusalem above!

"PRECIOUS IN THE SIGHT OF THE LORD IS THE DEATH OF HIS SAINTS."

DEAR to Thee, O Lord, and precious,
   Is the death of all Thine own;
Thou hast said, and we believe it,—
   Yet we weep and make our moan
When a soul, through Christ forgiven,
   Every grief and peril past,
All the toilsome journey ended,
   Rests with Thee, our God, at last!

Ah! our eyes are dim and blinded,
   Mists of earth hang heavily;
Where the stream of life is flowing,
   Only shades of death we see.
Here, our stars of hope have vanished,
   All our music died away;
While a welcome peal is ringing
   Yonder, in eternal day.

Yes, for thee that welcome sounded,
　　Dear one, through the courts on high,
When thy God and Saviour called thee
　　To His presence in the sky.
Gentle, dove-like sister-spirit!
　　Sweetly didst thou rise, and go,
Where thy heart had long been dwelling,
　　With thy Lord, so loved below.

And as here that love celestial
　　Ever reigned within thy breast,
Surely earthly love continues
　　In thy home among the blest.
Surely *we* are still remembered!
　　All is past of grief and gloom;
But, by founts of life eternal,
　　Love, a fadeless flower, shall bloom.

Joy of full and free salvation,
　　All the joys of home are there!
Oh, thou gracious, great Redeemer!
　　When we hope such joys to share,
Shall not heart and soul united
　　Raise the hymn of praise to Thee,
For the countless blessings purchased
　　By Thy grief and agony?

Dear to Thee, O Lord, and precious,
    Is the death of all Thine own!
On our darkness hath the dawning
    Of Thine Easter morning shone.
Through our tears the bow of promise
    Shines around with cheering ray,
While we journey to the country
    Where all tears are wiped away.

PARTING FROM TWO YOUNG FRIENDS.

Break not this heart, my children, with your weeping!
    On earth we can but meet to part again;—
I know it well; and yet, when life was younger,
    How often *I* have loved and wept in vain!

Now I look back upon a lengthened journey—
    The graves of many friendships mark the way:
I fondly thought them formed to last for ever,
    And saw them fade like rose-wreaths of to-day.

Yes, one by one, the flowery bonds were severed;
    The rainbow colours faded, gray and cold;
And grief was gentler far, and tears less bitter,
    When Death, not Time, unclasped the tender hold.

O life and love! O bliss dear-bought by anguish!
    Is there no refuge for the soul at last—
No comfort less imbittered, more abiding,
    Than these vain memories of joys long past?

Not so! One Heart, with love eternal glowing,
    One Friend who changes not, draws gently near;
Like the blue vault above, His arms surround us—
    His words of hope and promise all may hear:—

"Come, weary souls, with all your love and sorrow!
    Come to the Father's house, the better land!
All ye have sought and lost, 'mid earthly shadows,
    Receive in light from Mine, your Saviour's hand."

Be comforted, my children, and go forward!
    Our faith can look beyond earth's griefs and fears;
Beside our Lord at last, with joy, not sadness,
    We shall look down on *all* the vale of tears.

THE FIRST STEP.

 The first step bravely done!
 Child, that is well! but now
Step after step thou must go on—
A path lies open to a goal unknown,
 Which none can tread but thou.

 All are rejoicing here
 With thee: another day
May come, when thou, in doubt and fear,
No praising voice, no loving helper near,
 Shalt take a lonely way.

 Ah! would that Love could see
 Flowers only on thy road!
But stony places there must be;
We learn by many a stumble, wearily,
 How the right path is trod.

Yet may one mighty Friend
  Unseen, be at thy side!
On Him let all thy trust depend,
And let Him choose thy path, and to the end
  Thy pilgrim footsteps guide.

Whither, and how? He knows—
  My fond heart cannot tell.
But if, through dangers oft and foes,
Still to His kingdom straight the pathway goes,
  All must and shall be well.

And, all thy journey o'er,
  When the last step shall come,
Thy grandmother, long gone before,
May gladly wait upon the heavenly shore,
  The first to hail thee home!

AN EVENING TALK.

" Why so late alone, my child,
    Lingering in the garden bower?"—
" Mother, all the air is mild,
    Calm and sweet the evening hour.

" See, the moon begins to rise;
    One by one the stars appear,—
Are they not like angels' eyes
    Looking down upon us here?

" Grandpapa, is *he* not there
    With the angels far away?—
Never with his silver hair
    Shall again his darling play!

" As I think of him on high,
    Wishes rise, so fond, so vain!—
O that I had wings to fly,
    Grandpapa, to you again!

AN EVENING TALK.

"I was praying, mother dear,
    When you called me, in the bower;—
Sometimes heaven seems so near!
    'Twas a peaceful, holy hour.

"'Jesus, blessed Lord!' I prayed,
    'Keep me from all evil free;
Through life's sunshine and death's shade
    Bring me home to rest with Thee!'"—

"Come to my embrace, my love!
    Ever thus believe and pray!
Doubt not you are heard above;
    Christ Himself 'Amen' will say.

"He, our blessed Lord in heaven,
    Bids us haste to meet Him there;
Wings to help us He has given,
    You have tried them—Love and Prayer.

"Loving, praying, by His hand
    Safely guided, richly blest,
We shall gain the happy land,
    Where with Him our dear ones rest!"

WORDS OF CHEER.

Doubt it not—thou too shalt come
   To the jubilee of love,
Where the children gather home
   To the Sabbath rest above ;—
Lift thy drooping head again ;
When hast thou believed in vain ?

Still believe—though dearest light
   Vanish from the earthly sky,
Faded all thy visions bright,
   All thy hopes in ruin lie,—
Still believe ;—eternal day
Soon shall gild the thorny way.

Weep no more : look up and see
   Saints on Canaan's happy ground ;
Sinners, mourners once, like thee,
   Yet the narrow path they found,

Leading through the desert sand
To their heavenly Fatherland.

Love Divine it was, whose might
    Drew them from a world of snares,
Called them out of sin's dark night,
    Made them sons of God, and heirs;
Gave the Spirit in their breast,
Pledge of everlasting rest.

And when faith and hope are low,
    Think not Love has then forgot;
Never let the promise go,
    He who gave it changeth not.
Think, whate'er thy sorrows be,
" Jesus lives, and loveth me!"

None who trust in Him are lost;
    He will surely write each name
In the number of the host
    Who through tribulation came,
And with them we soon shall share
All the Shepherd's tender care.

Then shall dear ones, gone before,
    Greet our longing eyes again;

Sin and error vex no more,
   Where, made pure from earthly stain,
Truth revealed to every eye,
All is love and all is joy.

Great Redeemer, we are Thine!
   This our glory is and song.
Guided by Thy hand divine
   All the darkest path along,
Each shall come, all dangers past,
To Thy marriage-feast at last!

"NOT ONE OF THEM IS FORGOTTEN BEFORE GOD."

A joyful child, long years ago,
While yet unknown were death and woe,

What bitter tears were those first shed
Over my dove or sparrow dead!

Then an old stanza brought relief,
It met and soothed my childish grief,—

"The loving Lord forgetteth none—
He knows where each of these has gone."*

Passed many a long and weary year,—
And still that voice I seemed to hear;

It came, as if from pitying Heaven
A message to my soul were given,

* " Der liebe Gott, der keins vergisst,
  Weiss wohl, wo Jedes blieben ist."
                                OVERBECK.

"NOT ONE OF THEM IS FORGOTTEN

When I have watched and wept beside,
While lovely infants drooped and died—

Babes, to their mother's heart how dear!
Who scarcely smiled or sorrowed here.

Through the dim past, how I recall
One, first and loveliest of all,—

Beautiful stranger! ah, how brief
Thy visit here, of joy and grief!

Then came, with his clear starry eyes,
The brother, who beside him lies.

Another,—far across the wave
Who found a birthplace and a grave, —

And one, fair child of pain and fear!
Whose sweet eyes never opened here.

Ah! were these only, must we say,
Drops, from Life's ocean cast away?

All vanished—gone! that slumber deep,
Was it in truth eternal sleep?

Or, shrinking from our tears and strife,
Did they awake to nobler life?

Who asks? who now, of all below,
But *one* fond heart, would care to know?

And when her grave is by their side,
Who shall recall they lived, or died?

Nay, the old comfort comes again,
Faith hears, and echoes back the strain,

Faith in His love, who called, and pressed
The little children to His breast,—

" Our loving Lord forgetteth none—
He knows where each of these has gone."

"IN EVERY THING GIVE THANKS."

1 Thess. v. 18.

Give thanks for all things, children of our God!
Thanks for a Father's smile, a Father's rod;—
    All things are in His hands,
    All do as He commands,
All for His people are in love bestowed.

To the pure spirit all things are made pure,
All things are welcome to the humble poor.—
    Sad heart, lament no more
    In anguish as before;
Rest in one love, one hope for ever sure.

Almighty, what shall separate from Thee?
If Thou speak peace, from whence shall trouble be?
    Who shall enslave again
    If Thou unloose the chain,
And with Thine own hand set the captive free?

"IN EVERY THING GIVE THANKS."

Dark clouds and tempest, praise God in the height!
Thunders and lightnings, ye exalt His might!
  The fearful midnight hour,
  When wildest storms have power,
Must it not *end* in blessed morning light?

Deep tribulation, sin, and grief, and care,
Conflicts of doubt, and anguish of despair,
  Death itself—all, His will,
  His purposes fulfil,
His instruments, to do or to forbear.

Dark night of death, Christ hath illumed thy shade!
Satan, destroyer, thou art captive made,
  Beneath His feet to bend
  What time He shall ascend
The great white throne, for judgment vast arrayed.

Sing, children of our God! On Thee we call,
Friend of our need, Restorer of our fall!
  Thy work is finished now,—
  To Thee all might must bow,—
Amen! Amen! we can give thanks in all!

FAREWELL TO A FOREIGN MISSIONARY.

    Now, in the peace of God,
      Brother, pursue thy way!
Not vain has been our meeting here;
Eternal fruit may yet appear
      From the seed sown to-day.

    Go, with our prayers and love,
      To greet the noble band,
Chosen of God, thy toils to share,
Where fields of promise, wide and fair,
      Await the reaper's hand.

    The blessing of our Lord
      On all your steps attend!
As on His witnesses of yore,
May of His gifts a wondrous store
      On every head descend!

Strong in the Saviour's strength
  For toil and conflict, go!
The Lamb who suffered once and died,
Is now the Lion on our side
  To vanquish every foe.

Fear not in danger's hour—
  Shrink not from grief or pain;—
Hark to the "joyful sound" afar!
See light gleam from the Morning Star
  On islands of the main!

And here—Have mercy, Lord!
  Does not *our* sun decline?
Yet gladly do we turn, and gaze
On other lands, where the bright rays
  Of a new morning shine.

Where all is strange and new,
  Brother, around thee,—there
Recall the old far distant shore,
And friends, thou must behold no more,
  With earnest thought and prayer!

Alike our conflict still—
  In quiet sunshine here,

Or where deep Pagan darkness lies,
Or the false Prophet's standard flies,
    The same great Foe is near.

One Strength, one Hope, is ours,
    One guiding Star we claim;
"Come quickly, Lord!" or here, or there,
Echoes to heaven *that* longing prayer,
    From every heart the same.

Soon from the East and West
    Together we shall come,
When the glad reapers hasten all,
Obedient to the Master's call,
    For the great Harvest-home!

HYMN.

WRITTEN FOR THE ZURICH HYMN-BOOK.

O Christ, my Life, my Saviour,
   My Comforter alone!
In life or death, for ever
   I would be still Thine own.
   For ever I am Thine,
O Thou my soul's Redeemer!
   For ever Thou art mine!

Thou didst go forth, to save us,
   Strong in Love's silent might,
Through all the hosts of Satan,
   Down into Death's dark night;
   Then, Conqueror of the grave!
Thou camest back victorious,
   Mighty a world to save!

HYMN.

Now all Thy saints departed,
  From sin and death set free,
Sing of Thy bitter sorrows,
  Thy glorious majesty.
  My soul would join their lays,
And swell the joyful chorus
  To her Redeemer's praise.

Though all of hope and promise
  On earth may pass away,
One source of joy unfailing
  Shall ever with me stay;—
  Christ lives, my portion sure!
Let what is mortal perish,—
  My treasures are secure!

Thou art my Life eternal,
  My Sun in darkest hour;—
My joy shall be for ever
  To sing Thy love and power;
  Here, amid foes and fears,
And soon in peace and safety
  Through long eternal years.

Yes, soon the weary pilgrim
  Shall reach the land of rest,

To praise Thee, my Redeemer,
  With all the ransomed blest.
  Call me, Lord, speedily!
How gladly shall I hasten,—
  The journey ends with Thee!

AN AUTUMN EVENING.

"Here, beside our tranquil stream,
    Sing, my child, an autumn song."—
"Father, you shall speak, and I
    Listen, as we walk along."—

"See, our fading forests glow
    Bright as garden flowers of spring!
Everywhere, on vale and hill,
    Life from death seems blossoming.

"Like the smile of dying saint,
    Nature smiles in her decay;
Peace, as of some holy eve,
    Breathes in all the air to-day.

"Sabbath eve! how sweet the thought!
    All our toils and conflicts past,
How shall weary souls rejoice
    In the heavenly rest at last!

AN AUTUMN EVENING.

"See, how gently drop the leaves,
    Calmly, softly, to their tomb,
As if lifeless things could share
    Hope of better life to come.

"Are not germs of future spring
    Hid those withered stems among?
Is there not a prophet-voice
    In the murmuring streamlet's song?

"Through creation's changes still
    Trace we the Creator's hand;
Out of death and darkness rise
    Light and life, at His command.

"We, like autumn leaves, must fall,
    By the tempest lowly laid,
Gaining heaven's eternal spring
    Only through death's winter shade.

"Yet, unlike the fragile flower,
    We may fade with hope and joy;
Faith in Christ, immortal hope,
    Death's cold frost shall not destroy.

"In the kingdom of His love
    Nothing perishes in vain;

From destruction He can raise
Life and loveliness again.

"And when all things are made new,
Then shall be fulfilled at last
All the longings, all the prayers,
Of the saints in ages past.

"' Father! hallowed be Thy name!
Let Thy kingdom hasten on!
Over earth, redeemed, renewed,
As in heaven, Thy will be done!'

"Now o'er all the Land of Hope
Falls the latest sunset ray,—
Earth and sky seem glorified
As with gleams of Heaven's own day.

"All the loveliness of death
We have seen—and Life's sweet voice
We have heard—now hasten home,
Trust our Father, and rejoice!

"Underneath His wings of love
We and all creation rest;
Deep in each believing heart
Is His seal of life impressed."

AFTER MANY FAREWELLS.

Long hast thou wept and sorrowed,
   Poor heart! now dry thy tears;
Behold, with light and comfort
   Jesus Himself appears.

All other hope must perish,
   All earthly props decay;
Then let the seed be buried,
   The husk be blown away.

Yet think not God has granted
   But to recall again,—
His gifts of love and goodness
   Shall ever thine remain.

The seed, before it flourish,
   Must low in darkness lie;
And Love, to live for ever,
   Must for a season die.

But those like thee, bereavëd
    Within earth's darkened home,
Are rich in many a promise
    And pledge of joys to come.

"Trust in my mercy ever,
    My people!" saith the Lord;
Hold fast in deepest sorrow
    That soul-sustaining word.

The harvest-day is hasting,
    The rest from toil and pain,
When those who sleep in Jesus,
    Shall come with Him again.

And, more than all the treasures
    That morning shall restore,
Himself, Himself shall meet thee,
    Thy portion evermore!

Then rest, sad heart, in patience,
    With this petition still,
"Lord, all these vacant places
    With Thine own fulness fill!"

GOLDAU.

I HAIL thee in thy sad and awful silence,
Great, solemn sleeping-place of Goldau's shade!
    Where the green Alpine heights to heaven arise,
    Or mirrored in the lake their image lies
Around the mighty grave-stones God has laid.

O Paradise on earth, fair Alpine valley!
Thou wert too fair for any stranger-land.
    But in no Eden man is long to stay,—
    We read the record on these rocks to-day
In Ruin's language, traced by God's own hand.

How sweetly echoed once the children's voices,
The shepherd's call, the "Rans des vaches" wild song,
    From Rigi's slopes and Ruffi's forests green,
    Which now look down on desolation's scene,
Where sounds of life and joy have ceased so long!

GOLDAU.

The traveller 'mid the ruins pauses sadly,
Looks at sweet summer beauty, seen afar,
   And longs, and listens, if some voice from heaven,
   Some pledge of love or hope can *here* be given,
Where life and death have waged such bitter war.

Ah, see the Cross on yonder hillock planted,—
There is the pledge, the token from above!
   There may our faith and hope revive again,
   God's word of promise doth unchanged remain,
"The mountains shall depart—but not My love!"

Yes, from the Cross a stream of life is flowing,
Divine Redeemer, since Thy latest sigh!
   Beside the countless graves of earth it flows,
   It murmurs through Creation's groans and woes,
Telling of hope, and love that cannot die.

For He, our God, smites not in judgment only,—
Love blends with all—on Goldau's awful day,*
   How many a sad heart was for ever blest,
   How many a pilgrim gained the heavenly rest,
In one wild hour of anguish and dismay!......

---

* September 2, 1806. [When these verses were written (about 1830) the traces of the catastrophe were of course much more marked than now.—Tr.]

And even here shall dawn a blissful morning,
When "the new earth" in beauty shines complete;
  The ocean-graves shall yield their dead again,—
  Thy rocky tombs, Goldau ! shall open then,
And round thy Cross a joyful band shall meet.

LAST PRAYERS.

    No crown, no palms for me!
These are for victors in the fight; but I
Have been the vanquished one in every field,—
Oh, Saviour! who hast hope for such revealed!
    Low at Thy mercy-seat behold me lie!

    Turn not Thy face away!
Deal not in wrath with Thine unworthy child!
Yes, I have sinned; yet there is grace with Thee—
Thou givest mercy, pardon full and free,
    To fallen wanderers on the desert wild.

    No thought of *triumph* now!
That dream is over—rest is all I crave;
A little peace, after such deadly strife,
Some leaves of healing from the Tree of Life;—
    A glimpse of hope and heaven beyond the grave!

And for what yet remains
Of my sad pilgrimage, grant, O my God,
Meek, humble faith, to suffer and be still;
Meekly to watch Thy hand, to do Thy will;
Humbly to bow beneath Thy chastening rod.

Dark stream of life, rush on
To the eternal ocean, full and fast!
If only o'er the waves may fly the Dove
Of heavenly peace, and beckon from above,
To where a pardoned soul shall rest at last!

"OUT OF THE DEPTHS."

Low at Thy feet my spirit lies,
I would look up into Thine eyes;
A sad child seeks the Father's smile,—
My Father! leave me not the while!

Forsake me not, amid the strife,
The toil and weariness of life!
Though all around may fail or flee,
My soul is safe, O Lord, with Thee!

And other souls, than self more dear,
Thou gavest me to watch for here;—
Ah, *Thou* must watch! my anguished care
Is almost ending in despair!

Thou knowest all the conflict hard,
From year to year the hopes deferred;
The longing sigh, as time wears on,
" O watchman! is the night not gone?"

"OUT OF THE DEPTHS."

How vainly have I wept and strove!
And, have I erred in prayer or love?
Thou canst not err; Lord, hear me still!
Teach me to know and wait Thy will!

By the sole merit of Thy blood,
Forgive our sins, O Lamb of God!
And when our foes and fears increase,
Grant us Thy patience and Thy peace.

If earthly hopes must prostrate lie,
If dearest ones must droop and die,
Over the ruins let some ray
Shine from the dawn of endless day.

And when the darkest hour comes on,
The way seems lost, the land-marks gone,
Show on Thy cross, in words of light,
"The morning cometh, after night."

Fondly I dreamed of perfect bliss
On earth; but now I wait for this,
Till buds of promised grace and love
Shall blossom in Thy home above.

Do all that seemeth good to Thee,
If only I at last may see,
Safe in Thine everlasting rest,
The children of my sorrows blest!

ON A DARK WINTER DAY.

Is fair Nature dying?
    This funereal pall,
Must it hang for ever
    Darkly over all?

Stormy clouds are hiding
    All the morning light;
Has the sun forgotten
    How to conquer night?

Must the frozen streamlet
    Silent still remain?
Shall the Summer blossoms
    Never smile again?

Hush, desponding spirit,
    Hush the dark surmise!
Light shall spring from darkness,
    Life from death shall rise.

ON A DARK WINTER DAY.

Still the sun is shining
    Bright behind the cloud;
Only thy dim vision
    Cannot pierce its shroud.

Nature, bound and buried
    Under Winter's reign,
Soon shall burst her fetters,
    Start to life again.

Silent streams, awaking
    From their icy sleep,
Through the vale shall murmur,
    Down the mountain leap.

Thousand buds already,
    Far beneath the snow,
Dream of Spring's soft breezes,
    Dream of Summer's glow.

"Learn, sad heart, our lesson,"
    Now they seem to say;
"Dream of Spring and sunshine
    Through *thy* wintry day."

Yes, amid thy darkness,
    Through the gloom and fear,

Love Divine is watching,
    Christ Himself is near.

Since in dying anguish
    Once He bowed His head,
Then arose as Victor
    From amidst the dead—

Now His tempted people
    Need despond no more;
All our foes He conquered,
    All our sins He bore.

Love and power unfailing,
    Life from death shall bring;
From the grave's dark winter
    Everlasting spring!

"A LITTLE WHILE."

John xvi. 16.

" A little while!" so spake our gracious Lord
  To the sad band around that sacred board,
      While His long-burdened heart
      Already felt the smart
Of His own Father's sin-avenging sword.

'Tis for thee, also, weeping, weary one;
  Hold fast the word of promise, and hope on!
      Thy Father's hand ordains
      All these thy griefs and pains,—
" A little while!" they shall be past and gone.

Ah, weep no more for earthly woes and fears;
" A little while!"—how short the time appears!
      The harvest-joy shall come;
      Within the eternal home
The seed shall ripen which was sown in tears.

"A LITTLE WHILE."

Have all the lights of love quite died away?
Has thy last star withdrawn its cheering ray?
  Till the sad night wears past
  Weeping and prayer must last;
But joy approaches with the dawning day.

Do friends misunderstand, or mock thy pain?
Hast thou too fondly trusted, loved in vain?
  The Faithful One and True
  Can blighted hopes renew,
And hearts long severed reünite again.

"A little while!" the fetters clasp no more;
The spirit, long inthralled, is free to soar,
  And takes its joyful flight
  On radiant wings of light,
To the blest mansions of the heavenly shore.

There end the longings of the weary breast,
The full inheritance of grace possessed;—
  Ride o'er the stormy sea,
  Poor bark! soon shalt thou be
In the calm haven of eternal rest.

"A little while!" look upwards, and press on!
Soon shall the troubled dreams of night be gone,
  The shadows pass away
  Before the abiding day;—
The Saviour comes, to claim and bless His own!

EVENING MUSINGS.

Ah, leave the lamp unlit a while!
  I love to watch departing day;
Still lingers here the sunset smile,
  It gilds the mountains far away:
But ever, as we gaze, it fades;
The forests darken in their shades;
And chiller, like a dying sigh,
The breeze of evening passes by.

Like rose-wreaths in the crimson light
  So lately glowed the mountain pines,—
Now all has faded; day to night,
  As conqueror, the field resigns.
The pale, cold peaks of silent snow,
Seem mourning vanished hills below;
While Fancy hears the vesper-bell
Of hope and resurrection tell.

The day which here so gently dies,
　Lives in a distant land again;
Darkness with us brings sunny skies
　To loved ones far beyond the main.
Like soothing hymns which mourners hear
Around the grave of one most dear,
Peace, with a holy, wondrous power,
Fills all my soul in this calm hour.

BE STILL!

Peace, be still,
Through the night of grief or pain!
Meekly bow, nor strive in vain;
Let thy God do what He will,—
Peace, be still!

Peace, be still!
Vain are plans and words of thine
To unfold thy life's design;
God's own voice explains His will,—
Peace, be still!

Be thou still!
If in love thy Father chide,
Cling the closer to His side;
Let Him chasten as He will,—
Be thou still!

BE STILL!

    Be thou still!
Let the great Physician deal
With thy case, to wound or heal;
Trust His never-failing skill,—
    Be thou still!

    Lord, my God,
Grant me quiet, trusting faith!
Point my way through life and death
With Thy sceptre, or Thy rod,
    Lord, my God!

    Lead me on,
Lord, my Shepherd! feed, uphold,
Guide the weak one of Thy fold;
Till the night be past and gone,
    Lead me on!

SPRING.

Voices of Spring, with what gladness I hear you again!
Praises to Heaven ascending from mountain and plain!
  I too would raise
   Humbly, an anthem of praise,
  Joining in Nature's glad strain.

Listen, my soul, to the chorus on earth and in air;
All things created the praise of their Maker declare!
  Shalt thou alone
   Silent, refuse to make known
  All the rich grace thou dost share?

Hath not the heavenly spring-time of hope come to thee,
From the long winter of error and sorrow set free?
  While its soft light,
   Stealing across the dark night
  Ev'n of the grave, thou canst see!

O Thou almighty, all-merciful Saviour and Lord!
Would that each feeling, each thought of my soul, could
    record
        All the deep love,
        Which, from Thy fulness above,
    Into this heart Thou hast poured!

Now let me praise Thee! Thou knowest how blindly
    and long
All Thy kind dealings I read and interpreted wrong,
        Murmured and wept,
        Wilfully wandered and slept
    In my rebellion so strong.

But as the cold frosts of winter dissolve and give way,
When on their surface the sunshine and soft breezes
    play—
        So from the heart
        Coldness and darkness depart
    Under Thy love's cheering ray.

Give me a harp! from the valley of tears let me join
Those who are singing above in the Presence Divine;
        Anthems of heaven—
        Praise from a sinner forgiven—
    Sweetly the echoes combine!

FALLING ASLEEP.

Long years ago, a child at home,
    Weary of play among the flowers,
How sweetly slumber used to come
    By mother's side, in evening hours,
Watched over by her gentle eye,
Soothed by her pious lullaby!

That voice is silent,—ah! how long!
    And, weary in a thorny way,
How oft my children's sacred song
    Has soothed my cares, at close of day!
I listened to the holy strain,
Till balmy slumber came again.

Life's evening shadows gather now,
    Soon the last sleep shall o'er me steal,—
All earthly voices hushed, do Thou,
    My Saviour! then Thyself reveal!
Through angels' music let my ear,
Falling asleep, *Thy* welcome hear!

FOR EVER WITH THE LORD!

1 Thess. iv. 17.

O sweet home-echo on the pilgrim's way!
    Thrice welcome message from a land of light!
As through a clouded sky the moonbeams stray,
    So on Eternity's deep shrouded night
Streams a mild radiance, from that cheering word,
"So shall we be for ever with the Lord!"

At home with Jesus! He who went before
    For His own people mansions to prepare;
The soul's deep longings filled, its conflicts o'er,
    All rest and blessedness with Jesus there;—
What home like this can the wide Earth afford?
"So shall we be for ever with the Lord."

With Him all gathered! to that blessed home,
    Through all its windings, still the pathway tends;
While ever and anon bright glimpses come
    Of that fair City where the journey ends,

Where all of bliss is centred in one word,—
"So shall we be for ever with the Lord."

Here, kindred hearts are severed far and wide,
   By many a weary mile of land and sea,
Or life's all-varied cares and paths divide—
   But yet a joyful gathering shall be;
The broken links repaired, the lost restored,
"So shall we be for ever with the Lord."

And is there ever perfect union here?
   Ah! daily sins, lamented and confest,
They come between us and the friends most dear,
   They mar our blessedness and break our rest.
With life we leave the evils long deplored,—
"So shall we be for ever with the Lord."

All prone to error—none set wholly free
   From the old serpent's soul-ensnaring chain,
The truths one child of God can clearly see,
   He seeks to make his brother feel in vain;
But all shall harmonize in heaven's full chord,
"So shall we be for ever with the Lord."

O precious promise, mercifully given,
   Well may it soothe the wail of earthly woe;

O'er the dark passage to the gates of heaven
　　The light of hope and resurrection throw!
Thanks for the blessed, life-inspiring word,
" So shall we be for ever with the Lord!"

THE END.

www.ingramcontent.com/pod-product-compliance
Lightning Source LLC
Chambersburg PA
CBHW032355230426
43672CB00007B/705